The Student Success Manifesto

The Guide to Creating a Life of
Passion Purpose, and Prosperity

Published by:

Extreme Entrepreneurship Education Corporation
120 Wall Street, 29th Floor
New York, NY 10005
http://www.successmanifesto.com

First Edition: June 2003

ISBN, 0-9740411-1-4

Every student should read this book! The Student Success Manifesto *is a framework for creating wealth by taking your passion and turning it into profit!*

> — **Mark Victor Hansen,**
> Co-author, *The One Minute Millionaire*
> Co-creator, #1 New York Times best-selling
> series *Chicken Soup for the Soul*®

What a bright, motivated, successful young man!Michael Simmons' Manifesto is sure to give you an edge on your classmates and a jump-start in life!

> — **Dr. Stephen R. Covey, author,**
> *The 7 Habits of Highly Effective People*

Michael's words grab at my core aspirations and inspire me to accomplish more than I ever dreamed possible!

> — **Troy Byrd, Co-founder, Bryant College,**
> Global Entrepreneurship Program

Michael is a terrific example of the powerful principles he espouses in his book. The Student Success Manifesto *highly complements the lessons I teach my own students.*

> — **Fernando Alvarez, Entrepreneurship**
> Professor, New York University

The Student Success Manifesto *goes beyond the traditional paths to success many of us are surrounded by. Dale Carnegie, Robert Kiyosaki, and Napoleon Hill have met their match with Michael.*

> — **Ryan Allis, VP, UNC Entrepreneur Club,**
> Founder, The Entrepreneurs' Coalition

Acknowledgements

This book is dedicated to all of the individuals and organizations who inspire youth to create and achieve their dreams. Without experiencing the powerful effects of these programs first-hand, I would not have been inspired to write this book. I would like to specifically recognize the organizations below. All of them have had major impacts on my life:

About the Author

At the age of 21, Michael Simmons has been a keynote speaker, workshop facilitator, and panel participant on the topic of youth entrepreneurship at conferences from California to Washington D.C. As a student at the Stern School of Business at New York University, an author, teacher, speaker, and award-winning entrepreneur, he is able to deliver a unique perspective that connects with young audiences.

Michael has written popular articles on student entrepreneurship that have been published by Entrepreneur.com, *College Bound Magazine* , and *Whizteens in Business* (a book on youth entrepreneurship). In addition, he is a National Foundation for Teaching Entrepreneurship (NFTE) Certified Entrepreneurship Teacher and conducts an entrepreneurship class with inner-city youth under the auspices of the Liberty Partnership Program.

Michael co-founded his first business, Princeton WebSolutions (PWS) when he was 16. *Youngbiz Magazine* rated PWS the #1 youth-run web development company in the nation for the year 2000. In addition, Michael has won the NFTE Youth Entrepreneur of the Year Award, the Fleet Youth Entrepreneur of the Year Award for New York City, and the East Coast Collegiate Entrepreneur Award for New York State.

Contents

Foreword by Steve Mariotti   i

Author's Preface   iii

Introduction   xv

PART I: EXTREME ENTREPRENEURSHIP DEFINED

1. Extreme Entrepreneurship Overview   23
2. Fall Forward with Calculated Risks   33
3. Leverage Your Assets to Create Value   47

PART II: EXTREME ENTREPRENEURSHIP APPLIED

4. Tangible & Intangible Assets   65
5. Have Your Assets Do the Work   75
6. The Six Core Assets   79

PART III: EXTREME ENTREPRENEURSHIP MODEL

7. Extreme Entrepreneur Model Overview   93
8. Decision Characteristics   97
9. Ramifications of Our Decisions   99

PART IV: EXTREME ENDEAVOR CURRICULUM

10. Self-Education   111
11. Extreme Endeavor Overview   113
12. The Extreme Endeavors   123

PART V: THE EXTREME ENTREPRENEURSHIP CHALLENGE

13. The Challenge   181
14. The Journey   183
15. Start Now   193

Foreword

An entrepreneurial way of thinking is one of the most valuable concepts you, as high school or college student, can learn. As both an entrepreneur and a teacher of entrepreneurship, I have seen it not only transform my own life, but the lives of the many thousands of students who have graduated from the programs of the National Foundation for Teaching Entrepreneurship (NFTE), the organization I founded in 1987 to bring small business start-up expertise to low-income youth. However, regardless of your economic background, or even if you think your life's work will not be in business as such, I feel certain that the "extreme" entrepreneurial mindset that Michael Simmons presents in this book will be of great value to you in fulfilling your goals and dreams.

I met Michael a little over a year ago, in January 2002. He was a NFTE Young Entrepreneur of the Year, the award we make annually to a few outstanding students selected from all our programs, nationwide. When Michael came to me to say that he wanted to take a semester off from college, and one of his goals was to "shadow" me at NFTE's headquarters in New York, I challenged the decision and said, only if he would promise to go back to school in the fall. He wouldn't make that promise but what he did do was show me a cogent, well-thought-out plan for what he intended to accomplish during this "time off" (or "time on" as he prefers to call it).

One of these projects was *The Student Success Manifesto*, an impressive achievement and one which I hope will find many readers. The principles Michael has laid out here can easily be integrated into your habits of thought. They will allow you to clear away the underbrush and focus on what is truly important to you. I believe you will encounter some life-changing concepts in this easy-to-read and inspiring book.

Steve Mariotti,
New York, February 2003

Author's Preface

I graduated from a high school with a graduation rate above 90 percent and where most students went on to college. During the past few years of living in New York City I have had the opportunity to teach a web design class to inner-city youth, speak at high schools in the city, and volunteer with the National Foundation for Teaching Entrepreneurship. Each of these experiences has broadened my world view and opened my eyes to a completely different way of life than the one in which I grew up.

One major realization I have had is that students from the area where I grew up and the students that I teach now have one major thing in common. A large percentage are not passionate about school and learning. There are, of course, great teachers and effective schools. However, in general, many students are disillusioned in some way. From my experiences I have noticed that students from middle- and upper-class backgrounds live in cultures where education and school are very important. Even if they don't enjoy school, many of these kids simply find a way to get good grades, if only for the sake of getting good grades. Although many may not agree with the grading system, they follow it because of external pressure. Low-income inner-city youth, on the other hand, often come from a peer culture where education is not as high of a priority. Thus, it is easier psychologically for low-income, inner-city youth to drop out of school.

Is the answer that inner-city youth are not as intelligent? According to dropout rates, grades, SATs, and other success indicators that schools create, the answer is yes. However, my experiences tell me differently. **The goal of this book is to help students self-educate and create their own measures of success *regardless* of the quality of their school system or social background.**

Earlier this year, I was watching a television program that gave inside looks at different cultures from around the world. One of these was a tribe in Africa. As part of the initiation right into society, all female adolescents had to have their hair pulled out (yes, I'm not talking about a hair cut). Each and every hair had to be ripped out of the adolescent's scalp by hand. Males had to wear gloves filled with stinging red ants for a specified period of time without crying. Many fainted from the excruciating pain. While these are traditions that may seem pointless from our perspective, the youths were filled with pride and did not ask questions; for, once they went through the process, they were "officially" adults.

My first reaction to the program was to think how ridiculous it was to go through such a painful process. My second was relief that nothing like it existed in America. However, over time I've come to realize that many of the rituals we have in America are similarly unquestioned, ridiculous, and painful.

You may wonder, "Why would children voluntarily go through so much pain?" While I do not have a definite answer, I can certainly take a guess. These youths are growing up in a culture where everybody has been following the same traditions for centuries. They have seen older acquaintances, friends, and relatives go through the same process with pride. They probably received pressure from their parents, both spoken and unspoken, about how important it is to go through the process. They may not personally know anybody who did *not* go through the initiations, but they might have heard rumors about how those people lived horrible lives. After a decade of this conditioning in a child's formative years, it might be unrealistic to expect anything but pride for going through the process. In fact, once they complete the experience, they might talk about how it shaped their lives and how important it was.

I would like to make the point that these types of rituals are alive and well within our own society. Our rituals may not hurt as much as your hair being pulled out or being stung by red ants but, over time, little by little, they may be even more damaging. The pain is spread out in small doses over long periods of time, until it is a way of life that we think is our own fault.

I've gone through fourteen years of a ritual we call "school." I started off in first grade, going from 8 a.m. through 3 p.m., Monday through Friday, September through June, with people my same age. Each year, I received new freedoms. In first grade, I didn't get to pick any of my classes but, in second grade, I was able to have the choice of taking art or music. By seventh grade, I was even allowed to choose a study hall. And now, as a college student, I must take many "required" courses and choose a "major" that is supposed to guide the direction of my entire career. If I choose to follow the ritual further, I will take a 40-plus hour a week job, start at the bottom in a company, work my way up, and retire when I'm 60 or so!

Unfortunately, somewhere along the line, we resigned ourselves to accepting the T.G.I.F. (thank God it's Friday, or thank God it's five) mentality. Somewhere along the line we became excited by things that we should always have, such as the ability to take courses we are interested in or take breaks when we want to.

The school ritual is so powerful and invisible, that students who get low grades or low scores think that they themselves are less smart or capable of achieving their dreams. This would be like the teenagers in the tribe in the African country thinking that the pain from the ants or their hair being pulled out is their own weakness. Even worse, students who are able to "fit in" by getting good grades or SATs, might be doing it for the wrong reasons. They may dislike school, but force themselves to do well anyway. And because they are told they are smart, they continue to invest in the system even more. People who follow the system assume that anybody who does not fit into it is worse off than they are. Unfortunately, this seems to be often true because students who did not fit into the system blame themselves or have low self-esteem as a result. However, students who do not fit into the system can excel.

Rituals you can ignore to excel

There are some regulations we are forced to respect. We call these *laws*. For example, you cannot buy cigarettes until you are 18 or alcohol until you are 21. However, there are other rituals that nobody has written a law about, yet we blindly continue to follow (see list below). In the case of some of these, ignoring them can improve our lives.

In each community or social group, rituals are different. In the communities I have grown up in, some of the rituals have been:

1. Be popular in high school.
2. Party on the weekends.
3. Get good grades on standardized test scores.
4. Go to a college ranked highly in *US News and World Report*.
5. Major in finance or accounting.
6. Get a job in investment banking, consulting, or a Big 4 accounting firm.

In the inner-city communities that many African-American males grow up in the rituals are quite different. According to Dr. Jawanza Kunjufu, author of *To Be Popular or Smart: The Black Peer Group*, the most popular career paths for African-American males living in inner cities are sports, entertainment, drug dealing. To be successful in each these career paths, requires following different rituals.

As students, we may find these rituals unappealing at first, but over time we forget how we really feel and what we really want. The following *Dilbert* cartoon is humorous, but it also shows how people accept the norm even if it is hurting them and are skeptical of anything that is different:

In the cartoon above, we see Dilbert and his colleague talking about how entrepreneurship, starting your own business, is very risky. When they hear that their company was bought by a major competitor whose

CEO says he/she will be "humane," they both get excited. This cartoon illustrates perfectly how people are more willing to accept a norm where a company being "humane" is an added benefit, but they are not willing to take the financial risk to start their own company where they would have the freedom to dictate when, where, how, with whom, and what they work on.

We've put so much of our life into the way we have been living, we begin to look down on people who are different. We begin to look down on people who do not go out to parties and dress a certain way, along with people who get bad grades, go to low ranking schools, take a semester off, get married early, become pregnant early, and so on depending on who you associate with. Thus there becomes this invisible pressure to just keep your mouth shut and continue doing what everybody else around you is doing. It is easier that way, right? Once in a while, we may get the feeling of wanting to do something different, anything different. However, someone— ourselves or someone close to us — quickly talks us out of it.

When does life based on what we're passionate about and what we think is important begin? Does it really ever begin for most of us? I think it begins when we begin to define success not by what other people think, but by what we think. It begins when we plan and pursue our own goals, values, and beliefs. Success begins when we are constantly willing to change our definition of success until it suits us. Success in life for each of us is different. In this book, I will attempt to show that being different and following your own path is a prerequisite to success in *life*.

I will also demonstrate, through stories, statistics, and examples that anybody can be successful regardless of how well they did in the school system. In fact, there are many people, ironically many of the most successful people in this country that did not go through the system, or originally performed very poorly, in the school system. These often unmeasured anomalies are included in the following statistics:

1. "Twenty percent of people who did not graduate college earn more than college graduates."[5]

2. "Over fifty percent of all CEOs for Fortune 500 companies had C or C- averages in college." [6]

3. "Sixty-five percent of all U.S. Senators come from the bottom half of their school classes." [6]

4. "Seventy-five percent of U.S. presidents were in the lower-half club in high school." [6]

5. "Over 50% of millionaire entrepreneurs never finished college."[6]

6. There is no correlation between high SAT scores, good grades and money according to the research done for Thomas Stanley's book, *The Millionaire Mind*.

Within these groups of people, are those who were able to follow their passion, make a lot of money, and make a large difference — a lifestyle many think is impossible. While the difference between societal success and individual success may seem small, in actuality the difference is large. Each end requires vastly different means. This book is for people who want to be part of the unique group who define success individually.

This book is divided into five parts. Each part plays a critical role in the process of helping you understand and apply the philosophy. I address and then readdress key concepts to ensure the reader fully understands new ideas when they are introduced. Below are overviews of what you can find in each of the five parts of the book:

PART I: EXTREME ENTREPRENEURSHIP DEFINED
Understand the key tenets of Extreme Entrepreneurship and why they are important in your life.

PART II: EXTREME ENTREPRENEURSHIP APPLIED
Understand how the philosophy can be applied to your life regardless of whether or not you choose to start a company.

PART III: EXTREME ENTREPRENEURSHIP MODEL
Our ability to make the best decision available to us plays a key role in our success. Use the Extreme Entrepreneurship model to evaluate your decisions and make better ones.

PART IV: EXTREME ENDEAVOR CURRICULUM

Apply Extreme Entrepreneurship to your life on a daily basis by creating your own curriculum of Extreme Endeavors. The Extreme Endeavors below are introduced and explained:

1. Starting and Running a Business
2. Scholarships/Awards/Competitions
3. Shadowing
4. Seminars/Conferences/Organization and Association Meetings
5. Strategic Volunteering
6. Mastermind/Junto/Salon
7. Informational Interviews/Mentors
8. Journaling
9. "Vuja Daze"
10. Investing in Real Estate to Live in
11. Saving Money
12. Investing Money
13. Taking Time Off
14. School
15. Jobs and Internships

PART V: THE EXTREME ENTREPRENEURSHIP CHALLENGE

Build up the motivation to begin your journey.

As this is an e-book I encourage you to alter your reading style to maximize the experience. Specifically, I recommend:

1. After each chapter, write down your ideas, questions, insights, and thoughts on a piece of

paper and or share them with others through email, the telephone, or in person.

2. As ideas come to you record them on a piece of paper or on the computer so you can research them on the Internet.

3. Copy and paste interesting passages in the book into a document you can review in the future.

Introduction

Claim your own at any hazard. — Walt Whitman

This book is for all those with a burning desire in their heart to achieve their highest potential. Unfortunately, we often ignore this desire for years, or sometimes a lifetime. We often let mediocrity into our life *just* for a visit. However, it usually stays long past its welcome until, at last, it is no longer a visitor but rather a permanent resident. We save everything we want to change about ourselves and the world for a tomorrow that never comes. We sacrifice our present moment for a future that doesn't exist. And this is how, over time, we settle down and slowly forget who we truly are and what we could become.

But greatness is there, within each one of us, waiting to be born.

Every once in a while we may get a fleeting glimpse of our dormant greatness. In those glimpses anything becomes possible. Fear turns into courage and confidence. "If" turns into "when." Boredom turns into passion, pessimism into optimism. We are lost in the flow of life.

Many people have been able to hold on to these glimpses and turn them into a way of life. People we consider geniuses, like Einstein, Leonardo Da Vinci, Gandhi, and Edison have embarked upon this journey. As a result, they formed the foundation of many innovations in modern life that we now take for granted. This ability to turn glimpses into a way of life is within each one of us.

It is my most sincere hope that readers of this book will catch a glimpse of their potential and hold on to it for the rest of their life. Extreme Entrepreneurship is a simple yet powerful philosophy through which this process is begun.

The vision of Extreme Entrepreneurship is to spark the entrepreneurial mindset among young people so they are motivated to plan and pursue their own goals and visions and become this century's agents for change.

A major presupposition of Extreme Entrepreneurship is that **success is a system**. This implies that anything one person can learn to achieve can be replicated and improved upon by anybody else. Too often we disassociate ourselves from people who achieve greatness. We forget that everything that lives within them also lies with in us. In short, Extreme Entrepreneurship assumes that we are all human and capable of creating and accomplishing incredible achievements. **Being successful is not a birthright; it is a human right available to us all.**

Before we begin this journey, we must take account of what we are up against. As we begin a new millennium, new technologies and trends are affecting our lives and careers. To thrive we must be aware of these new changes and navigate our way through them. Among them are the following:

1. **Accelerating Change.** Technology is evolving at an accelerating rate, causing everything else to change at an increasing rate as well. Bill Gates, of Microsft, has said that "Business is going to change more in the next ten years than it has in the last fifty." Ray Kurzweil, author of *The Age of Spiritual Machines,* predicts that the next 100 years will be equivalent to the past 1,000 in terms of change. What took John Rockefeller decades to create takes people like Michael Dell (Dell) and Bill Gates a fraction of the time.

2. **Large ≠ Safe.** Large companies like Enron, WorldCom and Kmart, worth billions of dollars, can go bankrupt just like any smaller company. "From about 1979 to 1994, Fortune 500 companies eliminated 47 million jobs (about 25% of the entire workforce)."[1] Pat Alea and Patty Mullins, authors of *The Best Work of Your Life,* write that "Times have changed. Really changed. There is no such thing as 'a career' as we have known it in the past. You can no longer depend on a steady job with regular promotions at the same company over a prolonged period of time. The conveyor belt that once hauled employees forward and upward has jerked to a halt, and the floor is littered with casualties."

3. **Your own path is safer than the conventional path.** The current path that many use — getting

good grades, participating in extracurricular activities, going to a highly ranked school, and getting a 'secure' job — is more risky and competitive than ever. More students competing for fewer jobs mean that the formula will work for a smaller and smaller percentage of people. At the Stern School of Business at New York University, the school that I attend, a large majority of the students are majoring in finance. According to people in the industry, a few years after graduation most of the students have either moved on to different careers or have been fired. People once spent a lifetime at one company. Now, on average, they spend only a few years.

In a 1953 study conducted at Yale University of 100 students, 90 did not have goals. Seven had never written down their goals, but had an idea of what they were. The last three had written down their goals and looked at them at least twice a day. Twenty years later those last three people were worth more than the other 97 combined.[2] Creating your *own* goals and following your own path can be very powerful.

4. **The respected becomes the expected.** In the 21st century, certain credentials will begin to matter less and less. Already we can see this with high school and college education. At one point, it was very rare to have a high school diploma or a college degree, and the people who received them were often from the "well-to-do" part of society. This transition from the respected to the

expected is now occurring with the master's degree. Having achieved this level of education once carried a lot of weight. Slowly but surely more and more people are getting a master's degree because they feel they have to. The same concept holds true with internships. Once upon a time, an internship was exemplary and unique. Now, more and more people have had them and internships have become devalued. Today students are working harder and harder just to compete at the same level!

5. **Paying dues is risky.** People who pay personal dues instead of financial ones by taking a job just for the money, and ignore passion and personal growth and development, are more at risk then ever. They will be surpassed by people who are passionate about what they do and constantly learning, growing, branding themselves, and networking.

In a study published in *Getting Rich Your Own Way*, 1500 middle class workers were asked about their career goals and were subsequently tracked for 20 years. Eighty-three percent made career decisions based on money. The other 17% chose their careers based on passion. At the end of the study, there were 101 millionaires. Ninety-nine percent of these came from the 17% who had chosen a passion-based career. The other 83% were in careers that weren't particularly fruitful in either passion or money.

The following three questions naturally flow from the above trends:

1. How do we position ourselves for this era of accelerating change?

2. How do we use change to our advantage?

3. How do we effectively blend passion, money, relationships, and making a difference into our life?

This book is an answer to these questions!

As you read on, I encourage you to make the book your own by taking notes in it, talking about the ideas with others, and recording your insights and observations in a journal. At the end of the book are instructions on how you can receive a free Extreme Entrepreneurship e-mail newsletter and how you can become actively involved in the movement in a way that is beneficial for you!

Part I:
Extreme
Entrepreneurship
Defined

*Do not go where the path may
lead, go instead where there
is no path and leave a trail.*

— Ralph Waldo Emerson

1

Extreme Entrepreneurship Overview

Over the last few years, I've spent thousands of dollars on seminars, conferences, and books related to personal development and growth. All of this time and money spent learning, combined with being a student entrepreneur, has resulted in my developing the Extreme Entrepreneurship perspective. This book boils down all the time I have spent into a framework for thriving in the present and future.

When I was in elementary school, I remember hearing a teacher say that the technological revolution over the past two centuries had not lead to an equivalent improvement in the quality of life. We had built technology that made it possible to fly to the moon and back, but many people still had not even learned how to control their emotions. From this realization, I began to observe how people who were older, richer or more educated did not necessarily have a higher quality of life. These disparities led me to ask myself: "Why is this and how can I change it?"

Trying to answer these questions has led me to explore ways of bettering my own quality of life. In high school, even though I knew in the back of my mind that money could not be the main goal, I still chose that path as the primary way to improve the quality of my life. I figured that once I had enough money I would have the freedom to be the way I wanted to be. A quote from one of Jewel's songs very much described me: "They say that money breaks you, but I still want to see." I read the biographies of entrepreneurs like Michael Dell, Steve Jobs, and Bill Gates to learn how they had created wealth. I researched what personal qualities and character traits financially successful people had, and incorporated the ones with which I agreed into my life. As I gained more success in terms of achieving my goals, I was noticing improvements in the quality of my life. Unfortunately, the improvements were not as great as I had hoped. Furthermore, I found my happiness being very susceptible to my external environment and the ups and downs of my life.

As a college student, I began to read and learn more about human potential and people who focused on ways of *being,* such as Mother Theresa, Gandhi, and the Dalai Lama. I learned more about Eastern philosophies, went to spirituality seminars, and attended large conferences relating to spirituality and business. These seminars, books, and conferences had a large impact on my life, but I still felt that something was missing. Many of the ideas sounded intriguing, but did not seem practical for me.

Chapter 1: Extreme Entrepreneurship Overview

The philosophy of Extreme Entrepreneurship brings together the strengths of everything that I learned, and removes the weaknesses that each philosophy had alone so that it can beneficially be applied to the lives of young people.

Extreme Entrepreneurship is a not a step-by-step guide on what to do and what not to do. On the contrary, it is a reality-expanding philosophy derived from my personal experiences as a student entrepreneur and my research on what makes individuals successful. Extreme Entrepreneurship is supported by statistics, facts, and stories of real-world young people who are succeeding. The information is given in a short and enjoyable fashion so that the philosophy can be incorporated into your life quickly and easily.

Put simply, Extreme Entrepreneurship is a framework for maximizing the value you add to yourself and others. The rest of the book will be spent building upon this definition.

Value can be defined as anything that helps a targeted individual or organization achieve goals, vision, and mission. Thus, value is different for different people and organizations.

The extreme mindset, also known as the entrepreneurial mindset, is often associated with entrepreneurs, but can be applied to anybody. The following characteristics give a rough idea of how the extreme mindset differs from the conventional one:

Conventional	Extreme
Reactive	Proactive
Ordinary	Extra-Ordinary
Minimizes risk	Takes constant calculated risks
Follows the rules	Knows the rules and breaks them when practical and ethical.
Unmotivated	Ambitious
Gives up easily	Persistent
Pessimistic	Optimistic
Unimaginative	Creative
Bureaucratic	Flexible
Indifferent	Passionate
Goes for status quo	Goes the extra mile
Balances	Blends
Take jobs for money	Take jobs for intangible assets
Resistant to change	Constantly raising the bar; comfortable being uncomfortable.
Self-doubt	Self-confidence
Bored	Curious

When the extreme mindset is applied to owning a business it has led to many of our society's innovations and new jobs. Ninety-five percent of all radical innovations are attributable to small business.[3] When the mindset has been applied by those working at a job, it has led to success both for the individual and the company. When the mindset has been applied to sports, it has led to people like Tiger Woods, who are constantly working to improve their game, even though they are already the best in the world. When applied to life, the extreme mindset can lead to new levels of happiness and success.

Extreme Entrepreneurship adds value to yourself and others through mutually beneficial exchanges.
Mutually beneficial exchanges are powerful because they create value. For example, a business provides a service/product at a profit. In other words, it is able to receive more value than it loses by selling a product. A consumer profits by buying a service/product when the value received is greater than the cost. Therefore, both sides win and value is created. The more mutually beneficial exchanges a business does the more value it creates for itself and its customers. Or as billionaire Adnan Kashoggi has said, "Doing well [in capitalism] is the result of doing good."

To understand this concept better consider the chart below. The two red, rounded rectangles represent the two stakeholders in a corporation. With each stakeholder, the corporation gives and receives value. The more value a company is able to provide its stakeholders, the more successful it becomes.

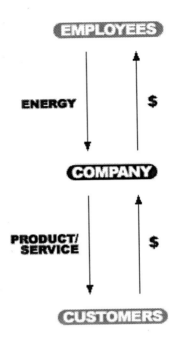

Many of the same concepts of giving and receiving value can be applied to us as individuals. Whether or not we realize it, we are constantly exchanging value with others. We simply have different stakeholders. Examples of these stakeholders could be the following:

1. Family
2. Friends
3. Community
4. Contacts
5. Mentors
6. Mentees
7. Employees (if you own a company)
8. Employer (if you work in a company)

The chart below illustrates the stakeholder concept for an individual.

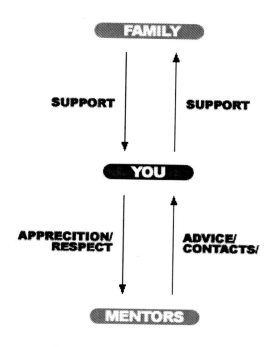

The value an individual receives can be anything that satisfies his or her needs and wants (goals). Below are more examples of mutually beneficial exchanges individuals may partake of:

Whom	Give	Receive
Friend	Advice / Support	Advice / Support
Contact	Introduction/ Relevant News	Introduction/ Relevant News
Employer	Time, Energy, and Experience	Money, Experience, Contacts, etc.
Family	Support	Support

Adding Value Through Assets

I define an entrepreneur as somebody who creates massive value for other people.
> — Mark Victor Hansen, Co-author,
> Chicken Soup for the Soul Series

In the section above, I mentioned the importance of adding value. In this section I will explain how you can add the most value with the fewest resources through assets. **Many of the world's richest individuals have added more value to more people through the assets they leveraged.** In his best-selling series of books, *Rich Dad, Poor Dad*, Robert Kiyosaki defines a financial asset as anything that puts money back in your pocket without you doing work. For example, ownership in a company is a financial asset because you earn money based on how well the company performs, not based on how many hours you work at the company. A way to acquire a financial asset besides buying it, is creating it. Henry Ford created a business enterprise (financial asset) that standardized the assembly line for cars and was able to offer the first affordable car to the public. Through this enterprise, the Ford Motor Company not only offered massive value to the public, but also to Henry Ford himself, the creator of the asset. When John D. Rockefeller was a young boy he lent a farmer $50 and later received the money back plus interest. Concurrently, he worked for a neighbor at a low wage doing backbreaking farm work. After realizing that he made more money with the money he lent and didn't have to **actually** work for, he vowed always to have money do the work for him. Applying this simple concept of having an asset do the work, Rockefeller went on to become the world's richest man.

Adding value to a lot of people is not as simple as it may sound. Think to yourself for a second. If you want to add value to a lot of people and make a large, positive difference in the world, what would you do? As students we often lack the assets to make large, measurable changes right away. Students generally have a limited amount of knowledge, contacts, money, and other assets. This makes it difficult to add a large amount of value in the present moment. Sure we have the power to do what we think is best at each moment. However, when it comes down to it, what Bill Gates could do with a sentence could take us years. In other words, **we all have assets that govern the value we can add at any given moment.**

Now that you have a basic understanding of Extreme Entrepreneurship (framework for maximizing the value you add to others and yourself), the next chapter will shed more light on the two prongs of the philosophy. An Extreme Entrepreneur leverages an extreme mindset and assets to create value. The word "extreme" is the mindset while "entrepreneurship" is how the mindset is applied

2

Fall Forward with Calculated Risks (Extreme)

It is not the critic who counts, not the man who points out how the strong man stumbled, or where the doer of deeds could have done better. The credit belongs to the man who is actually in the arena; whose face is marred by the dust and sweat and blood; who strives valiantly; who errs and comes short again and again; who knows the great enthusiasms, the great devotions and spends himself in a worthy course; who at the best, knows in the end the triumph of high achievement, and who, at worst, if he fails, at least fails while daring greatly; so that his place shall never be with those cold and timid souls who know neither victory or defeat.
— Theodore Roosevelt

Following the norm has become more risky than ever. Accepting a job only for the money and as a result not learning much and not being passionate, is a great risk. We must be willing to take calculated risks, diverge from the norm. If we do happen to fall, we must fall forward, utilizing what we learned from the fall to take another calculated risk. By consistently taking risks and falling forward, we put the probability of hitting it big in our favor and make constant progress. The following chart illustrates how falling forward with

Part I: Extreme Entrepreneurship Defined

calculated risks can be less risky than not taking any risks at all:

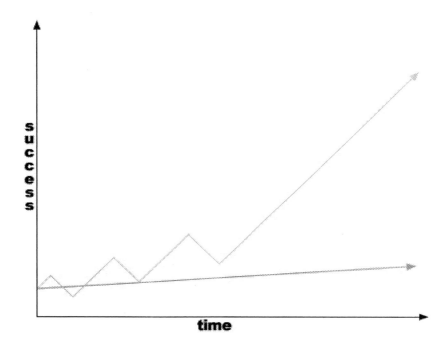

While this chart is generalized and not accurate for everyone, it makes the following points:

1. The red line, the more conventional path moves slowly and steadily. Fifty years ago, this path of getting good grades, going to a good college, and getting a good job had a much steeper curve. As society changes, this conventional path will become less and less steep. With the recent downturn in the economy, many individuals who "paid their dues" were frustrated that they had given so much time to

34

their company but were now unemployed. In other words, their steady line took a downturn and they had little to show for years of work. Or consider that taking the conventional path of going to college and getting a masters degree is becoming more and more expensive and less and less of a credential, because more people are going school and taking this route.

2. The green line represents the Extreme Entrepreneur path of taking calculated risks to fulfill your dreams. In the short term, taking this path is often difficult and hard to see results from. It may seem to be the wrong choice at first. However, over time, as you invest in your tangible and intangible assets, even when you fall you will still be more successful than those taking the more conventional path. If you are always aiming big, you always have the possibility of hitting it big. And, over time, maybe after you have fallen a few times, you may do so.

Calculated Risk is Less Risky than No Risk

Research by scholars at the Federal Reserve and the Internal Revenue Service has found that the net worth of the top one percent of Americans is greater than that of the bottom 90 percent.[4] With money as well as with other indicators, it is clear that success does not lie in taking the road most traveled. **To be in the top .0000001% of anything, you cannot follow the road most taken.**

The good news is that the road *less* traveled on is paved with our dreams and is available to us *all*, regardless of the barriers we often let stop us. While performing research for his best-selling book, *The Millionaire Next Door*, Thomas Stanley found that more than 80% of millionaires accumulated their own wealth and did not inherit it. In other words, most financial success in America is not determined by where we start out, but what path we choose to take. Unfortunately, we often pass by the path paved with our dreams because we are skeptical of our ability or of the opportunity or because we consider the road too risky. If only we could see Gandhi when he was a teenager, or Bill Gates when he was first learning about computers, then we would know that, no matter how much people achieve, they were once just *ordinary* kids without superhuman powers. At some point they decided to take the road less taken — and so can we.

A person following the conventional model and choosing the conventional path depends on the system. They *need* the high grades, to go to the college they want. An Extreme Entrepreneur leverages the system and focuses on activities that provide the most value. Consider these supporting statistics, which I now repeat for emphasis:

1. "Twenty percent of people who did not graduate college earn more than college graduates."[5]

2. "Over fifty percent of all CEOs for Fortune 500 companies had C or C- averages in college."

3. "Sixty-five percent of all U.S. Senators come from the bottom half of their school classes." [6]

4. "Seventy-five percent of U.S. presidents were in the lower-half club in high school." [6]

5. "Over 50% of millionaire entrepreneurs never finished college."[6]

6. There is no correlation between high SAT scores, good grades and money according to the research done for Thomas Stanley's book, _The Millionaire Mind._

With the conventional model that most of us are taught, you have to graduate college and get good grades to be successful. In the Extreme Entrepreneurship model graduating college and getting good grades can help you, but you are _not_ dependent on them. The statistics above are normal in the reality of the Extreme Entrepreneur.

In the conventional model averages are the norm. You might hear, "If something is true for 70% of the people, then it must be true for you." In the Extreme Entrepreneurship model averages are for average people. If you want to be with the .0000001% of people who are very, very rich or the .0000001% of people who achieve greatness in specific areas, than the averages often will not apply to you. **Averages should not**

discourage you from taking the road less traveled upon and following your heart.

Successful College-Age Individuals

Successful Extreme Entrepreneurs are made not born. Anybody can become one. If you think you are too young or not educated enough to achieve your wildest dream, then think again. Considering the following excerpt from a study on the founders of *Inc. 500* companies (http://www.inc.com/inc500), America's fastest growing private companies:

> *Forty percent of the Inc. 500 founders had no experience in the industry they were entering…Over one-third of Inc. 500 founders were out of work when they started their companies, many others had just a few years on the job. These entrepreneurs have few if any contacts in the field they are going to enter…It is their personality, adaptability, and their willingness to provide specialized products or services that wins the day, rather than traditional industry expertise they bring.*

I've met dozens of students who are Extreme Entrepreneurs, and doing well in school is definitely not a prerequisite of success (although it can certainly help). If you think that just because you did not get into a highly ranked school, or just because you have been getting lower average grades, you won't succeed, think again. Being a successful Extreme Entrepreneur is based on a different set of standards that school does not necessarily teach or measure. If entrepreneurs had to be book smart, then people who were still in college would not be able to create more successful businesses than people 20 years older. Yet they can. Some examples of businesses started by young people either in school, or just out, are:

Microsoft (http://www.microsoft.com)
Bill Gates (with Paul Allen) after leaving Harvard as junior.

Dell (http://www.dell.com)
Michael Dell, while attending the University of Texas.

Napster (http://www.napster.com)
Shawn Fanning, while attending Northeastern University.

Netscape (http://www.netscape.com)
Marc Andreesan, while attending the University of Illinois.

Hershey Foods Corporation (http://www.hersheys.com)
Milton Hershey opened his first candy shop in 1876 at 18 years of age. It failed six years later, but he hit gold ten years after that when he founded the Lancaster Caramel Company. The Hershey Food Company later became a subsidiary.

Federal Express (http://www.fedex.com)
Fred Smith was attending Yale. He wrote a business plan for Federal Express and was given a "C" by his professor.

Nantucket Nectars (http://www.nantucketnectars.com/)
Tom First and Tom Scott, after graduating Brown. In 2001, Nantucket Nectars had $66 million in revenue.

Apple (http://www.apple.com)
Steve Jobs (with Stephen Wozniak), after leaving Reed University.

Tripod (http://www.tripod.com)
Bo Peabody, while attending Williams College. Later sold it to Lycos for $58 million.

TheGlobe.com (http://www.theglobe.com/)
Stephan Paternot and Todd Krizleman attracted a $20 million investment while attending Cornell. The company later went public.

Vivendi Universal (http://www.vivendiuniversal.com/)
Barry Diller, after dropping out of the University of California at Los Angeles, became the unofficial head of programming for ABC by the time he was 23. He is now the CEO of Vivendi Universal.

Virgin (http://www.virgin.com/)
Richard Branson dropped out of high school, started a magazine, and then later went on to start the Virgin "empire."

Lillian Vernon (http://www.lillianvernon.com/)
Lillian Vernon started her mail order business with a $2,000 wedding gift. At the time, she was 21, pregnant, and a housewife. In 2001, revenue was $287 million.

Rolling Stone Magazine (http://www.rollingstone.com/)
Jann Wenner, a University of California at Berkeley drop-out, founded his magazine at 21.

Def Jam (http://www.defjam.com)
Rick Rubin, while attending NYU. He collaborated with Russell Simmons and produced such artists as Run D.M.C., Beastie Boys, and L.L. Cool J. and became a millionaire.

Yahoo (http://www.yahoo.com/)
Jerry Yang, while attending Stanford.

IDT (http://www.idt.com)
Howard Jonas, after dropping out of Harvard, founded IDT, which had a market capitalization over $1 billion as of late 2002.

Motion Picture Director
Steven Spielberg dropped out of California State University, Long Beach. He finally graduated 33 years later in 2002 with a degree in Achaeology.

Nike (http://www.nike.com)
Phillip Knight, while attending Stanford.

Anthony Robbins Companies (http://www.tonyrobbins.com)
Anthony Robbins never attended college and started a company called Achievement Enterprises, where he had 15 employees by the time he was 20. He later went on to create a self-development "empire."

Domino's Pizza (http://www.dominos.com)
Tom Monaghan tried college six times but never got past his freshman year. In 1960, at 19, Tom borrowed $500 and purchased a pizza store called DomiNick's. Four years later, he renamed the company Domino's Pizza.

Hewlett-Packard (http://www.hp.com)
After leaving Stanford, William Hewlett and David Packard started HP out of a garage.

Princeton Review (http://www.review.com)
John Katzman, soon after graduating Princeton.

Digitas (http://www.digitas.com)
Michael Bronner, while attending Boston University. He founded the company from his dorm room in order to help pay his tuition. Digitas is as of this writing a public company.

TakingITGlobal.org and Buybuddy.com
Michael Furdyk sold his first business for $1 million when he was 16. After graduating high school, he received $5 million in venture capital to found Buybuddy.com and co-founded TakingITGlobal.org. As of the writing of this book, Michael is only 20 years old.

Pinpoint Networks (http://www.pinpoint.com)
Jud Bowman, while in high school. Pin Point was named "Top 10 Wireless Companies to Watch" and has over 30 employees as of this writing.

Donald Trump
Donald took over his father's business and closed his first major deal when he was 22. The rest is history.

Hard Candy (http://www.hardcandy.com)
Dineh Mohajer, while a pre-med student at the University of Southern California, was pushing $10 million in sales within months of starting her company in 1995. It was acquired by Louis Vuitton Moet Hennessey in 1999.

Subway (http://www.subway.com)

Fred Delucca while struggling to pay for college borrowed $1,000 from a family friend to open his first sandwich shop.

Sharkbyte and Powerdime.com (http://www.joshuanewman.com)

Joshua Newman started and sold two Internet companies while attending Yale. Currently, Josh is running an indie film production company.

Polaroid Corporation (http://www.polaroid.com/)

Edwin Land took two leaves of absence from Harvard. During the first leave of absence, he created a new kind of polarizer, which he called Polaroid. During the second leave of absence he started a laboratory with other young scientists.

CNN (http://www.cnn.com)

Ted Turner was kicked out of Brown twice, before taking over the helm of his father's failing billboard business when he was 24. He expanded the business into television. Turner used the profits from the company to launch CNN, the first 24-hour all-news cable channel.

Kinko's (http://www.kinkos.com)

Paul Orfalea, while attending the University of Southern California. The following is an excerpt about him from Seth Godin's, *Survival Is Not Enough*:

Paul is profoundly dyslexic. He didn't learn how to read until he was well into elementary school and did nothing in high school that would be associated with the idea of success. He went to college but didn't care an awful lot about his classes. It was the perfect background for an entrepreneur.

Paul started a little copy shop (so little he had to wheel the machine outside to make room for customers) on his college campus. He sold pens and paper and made copies. That store grew to become Kinko's, a chain with more than one thousand outlets that he was able to sell for more than two hundred million dollars to an investment group.

I bring up these profiles not to show that school is unimportant. On the contrary, I think it can be beneficial to many students when leveraged. My goal is to show that *anybody* can achieve anything. I hope that the statistics and real world examples I have brought up will give you the confidence to follow your dreams.

3

Leverage your Assets
to Create Value
(Entrepreneurship)

Try not to become a man of success but
rather try to become a man of value.
— Albert Einstein

What is entrepreneurship? This may sound like a simple question, but there are many answers. The word is derived from French and came to mean, "Taking on risk." However, over the years as society has evolved, the word entrepreneur has become very closely associated with a person who chooses to start his or her own business. According to today's dictionaries it means, "A person who organizes, operates, and assumes the risk for a business venture."

When America was founded a fairly large percentage of the population owned farms, which served as their business. According to Robert Kiyosaki, "Just 100 years ago, approximately 85% of the U.S. population was either independent farmers or small shopkeepers."[7] However, as America's economy developed, we moved into an industrial society in which most of the people became employees and that is where we have remained, until now.

Amidst the ups and downs of the economy, we are undergoing a major shift in the way we live. Who we are as individuals is changing. Instead of working our entire life at one job, we are working, on average, only a few years with one company. A secure job is no longer guaranteed to even the best educated. Opportunities will be mainly available for people who are prepared for them and capitalize on opportunities. If we want to succeed we can't wait for somebody to give us what we want. We must take control of our lives. We are free agents and must take ownership and realize that we are all running a company called Me, Inc.

Me Inc.

We are CEOs of our own companies: Me Inc. To be in business today, our most important job is to be head marketer for the brand called You.
 — Tom Peters

A business enterprise is a financial asset. An entrepreneur creates the system and then has the ability to stop working on it and still receive money through ownership of the asset. We as individuals are human enterprises, and just like a business, we have assets. We can take ownership and receive the benefits of these assets, by recognizing and leveraging them to create value for ourselves and others. I will explain how this can be done later on in the book.

One of the major reasons that approximately 80% of millionaires are entrepreneurs is because of leverage. The entrepreneur has created a system that makes it possible to receive passive income, wealth that the entrepreneur does not have to work for. Using leverage such as employees and branding, the entrepreneur can become rich while he or she is asleep. In the same way that a business leverages its assets, we too as individuals can leverage our own tangible and intangible assets. These include:

1. Money
2. Brand
3. Health
4. Relationships
5. Self-Development
6. Personal Growth

The Extreme Entrepreneur is a person who organizes, operates, and assumes the risk for his or her own *life*. He or she is an individual who takes control and accountability and leverages his or her tangible and intangible assets to create a life of prosperity with an extreme mindset.

The Extreme Entrepreneur Quadrant

Extreme Entrepreneurs think about maximizing values by choosing to do the highest value activities *and* by choosing to the highest value ways of being. Let me explain. A conventional entrepreneur may start a business system, but not use an empowering mindset. This might result in not taking proper care of one's health, getting stressed every day, yelling at employees and alienating customers. An Extreme Entrepreneur understands that there is value both in becoming an entrepreneur and managing one's life effectively with an extreme mindset. On the other end of the spectrum, an individual may have an extreme mindset yet invest in limiting activities. The chart below boils down the four quadrants of being and doing. Each choice you make will help determine which quadrant you invest in.

ACTIVITIES

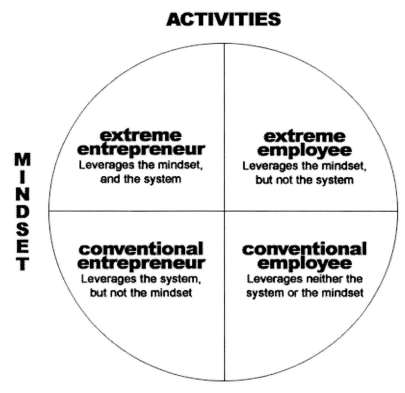

Whenever we make a choice we have the ability to control ourselves and/or our activities. Below are definitions for each word introduced in the quadrant. Keep in mind that these definitions do not necessarily mirror their common definitions. For example, an employee is not defined as somebody who works for a company in Extreme Entrepreneurship. An employee is someone who is leveraged by a system. On the other hand, an entrepreneur creates and leverages that system. For example, an individual can be an Extreme Entrepreneur by maximizing a relationship with a friend or choosing to eat healthily. In other words, in Extreme Entrepreneurship an Extreme Entrepreneur and a Conventional Entrepreneur are not necessarily business owners. Lastly, every second one must choose whether to be an Extreme Entrepreneur. One simply isn't an Extreme Entrepreneur by starting a business or going to a great school. It is an ongoing process of decision making.

The tables below explain what each of the words in the chart above mean. One of the tables was used earlier in the book, but is important to see again.

CONTROLLING YOURSELF	CONTROLLING ACTIVITIES
Extreme – Adopting a way of being that you choose.	**Entrepreneur –** Choosing activities that align with your vision and goals.
Conventional – Adopting the common way of being.	**Employee –** Going along with the activities that come up.

Part I: Extreme Entrepreneurship Defined

Employee	Entrepreneur
Told where to work	Chooses location
Told when to work	Chooses hours
Told who to work with	Chooses partners, customers, & employees
Told what to wear and how to interact	Chooses what to wear and how to interact
Dependant on the system	Leverages the system
Told what to work on	Chooses what to work on and what to delegate
Bears personal (growth and development, networking, branding) risk	Bears financial risk
Dependant on tradition	Dependant on change
Works on somebody else's vision	Recruits others to help work on his or her vision
Has work delegated by others	Delegates own work

Conventional	Extreme
Reactive	Proactive
Ordinary	Extra-Ordinary
Minimizes risk	Takes constant calculated risks
Follows the rules	Knows the rules and breaks them when practical
Unmotivated	Ambitious
Gives up easily	Persistent
Pessimistic	Optimistic

Unimaginative	Creative
Bureaucratic	Flexible
Indifferent	Passionate
Supports status quo	Goes the extra mile
Balances	Blends
Take jobs for money	Take jobs for intangible assets
Resistant to change	Constantly raising the bar; comfortable being uncomfortable.
Self-doubt	Self-confidence
Bored	Curious

Intangible Assets Are More Important than Tangible Assets

I recently had a conversation with a soon-to-be graduate of NYU working on Wall Street. I was able to catch him in the school computer lab around 8:00 pm on a Monday while he was on a work break checking his personal e-mail. He said that his boss was very rude and yelled at him at least once a day. He also said that this was okay because this was how his boss and his boss's boss were once treated. He further went on to say that if he made one mistake he could be fired. With this sort of dependence on traditions that may or may not work, these types of employees will be unprepared for change and afraid of taking risks in the future.

After they graduate, many students are willing to sacrifice years of their life in employment situations where they are not enjoying themselves. In return, these people often have a higher salary in the short term. However, there are hidden costs to this.

Part I: Extreme Entrepreneurship Defined

Although an employee may receive a higher salary than an extreme entrepreneur in the short term, an Extreme Entrepreneur has more control over intangible assets such as knowledge, growth, brand, and networking. The Extreme Entrepreneur can focus on what he or she is most passionate about. A salaried, conventional employee may be doing highly paid "busy work" while the Extreme Entrepreneur is able to constantly learn, grow, and network. An Extreme Entrepreneur invests in intangible assets that may take awhile to pay off financially, but in the long run these assets have the potential to be extremely lucrative. Each asset is a hedge against risk.

Below is the story I was told by Scott Pollack, a student at the Stern School of Business, who had a pivotal experience working at a startup:

> *A few weeks before my high school graduation, I found a classified ad in a weekly Internet industry e-mail newsletter (The Silicon Alley Reporter) by an Internet start-up looking for a Junior Web Developer. I was going to attend NYU in the fall as a computer science major, and had significant interest and experience in programming, so I submitted my resume via e-mail. I got a call soon after by the then-CEO. Halfway into a phone interview, he paused and said, "Wait a minute, how old are you?" I said, "18." He said, "You're f***ing 18?!" Apparently, he had overlooked my age on my resume, so he told me that they were looking for someone older and with more experience for the position. However, he said I should come in to the*

office anyway. One day after ninth-period calculus, I took the train from Long Island into New York City to meet the only two employees of the firm (a CEO and a President). From that meeting I was offered a summer internship, and so it all began.

When I arrived, in July of 1999 (I had to delay my start date so I could attend my senior prom), I was one of four: the CEO, the President, and two interns. The company had $1.1 million in seed funding from an angel investor. The company did not become profitable for almost two years (it required a significant change in its business model first), but while I was there I did not think through any of the risks. I believed without a doubt that I was working at the next Microsoft. There was no doubt in my mind that I was going to be a millionaire before my 21st birthday. Of course, my mind was clouded by stories of my Internet industry colleagues making billions overnight.

Even though my stock options are worthless, working at this start-up was the cornerstone of my professional career. **The lessons learned while working there are worth far more than the millions of dollars I had originally sought after.**

The original business model of the company was to be a broker of intellectual property, purchasing patents from universities and government research labs, and then licensing them for a profit. My original responsibilities were to review patents that were under consideration, to try to understand the technology, and to give my impressions as to the *potential for future uses. That, of course, was in addition to running to Kinko's and cold calling potential clients. I started out at $10 an hour.*

During that first summer, I also sat in on meetings with web developers to learn more about the web portal that we were planning to create as the foundation for the business operations. While the web development firm we hired was constructing the site, I tried to learn as much as possible about the site design, and eventually began tinkering with the code. When the heads of the company saw that I was working faster than the developers were, and was finding flaws in their code, I became responsible for all web development projects. By February of 2000, I had complete control over the website and became the go-to guy for anything technical. As the company grew, I worked with the Director of Business Development to forge relationships with other companies. When we met, I would analyze the technological feasibility of partnerships, etc. After a year or so at the firm, I went to the CEO of the company and said "Hey, how about a new title? 'Intern' is getting kind of old." That is how I become the Chief Information Officer (CIO).

The job of CIO was stressful, especially for a college freshman. Since the economy was booming, and dot-com CEOs were practically rock stars, I concentrated almost exclusively on working. School took a back seat to my job, and my grades definitely felt the effect. On the other hand, working at the start-up was the most significant learning experience of my life. The connections I made and the experience I gained are worth ten more C's in my freshman literature class.

I was compensated with raises. I peaked at $20 an hour. I was offered a salary but I declined, as I thought that would add too much pressure. My stock options were never exercised.

While I was at this start-up, I was able to learn about more than just my role in the company. In addition to the technical skills I gained, I learned three major lessons:

1. *Companies are not well-oiled machines.*
2. *Business is the ability to work with people, not just numbers.*
3. *Bigger is not always better when it comes to company size.*

My work at the startup is what inspired me to change my major from computer science to business. Also, I learned to how to think critically. Since I had to wear many hats, I constantly faced new challenges. Often I would be working alone on projects, so when I had a question, I had nowhere to turn. At those times, I could be found in the computer section at the local Barnes & Noble researching possible solutions to problems. I have been able to transfer those skills to all of my pursuits in business. These are all lessons I would have never learned by being just another cog in a large company.

Working at a small company during an economic boom was great. Everyone is happy, phones are

> *ringing off the hook, and everyone's future looks bright. But when things take a turn for the worse, it is easy to get frustrated. Everyone wants to work for the next Microsoft, but no one wants to stay at a company that does not seem to be going anywhere. Nonetheless, I firmly believe that I learned just as much in bad times as I did in good times.*
>
> *I have no regrets about my startup experience. In addition to helping me develop my soft skills, it was an integral part in my development of a career path in business. I often wonder where I would be if it were not for one small ad in the* Silicon Alley Reporter.

As we have seen in Scott's story, the majority of the benefits he received were intangible. Unfortunately, people tend to choose the path with the largest number of "visible " benefits and marginalize the importance of "invisible" benefits. As a result, in choosing a job or internship, many choose to work with a company with a good brand name that provides $12 an hour instead of accepting $10 an hour at a smaller, perhaps unknown company. We can see how much Scott learned and enjoyed his position. Although the company he worked for does not exist anymore, he was able to get promoted from an intern to the Chief Information Officer in about a year.

Young people generally have more limited options as to where they can work. Generally, if we want to work in a large company that has a good name, we have to start at the bottom and work our way up. As a result, we lose many "unseen" benefits. Large companies certainly have many benefits. For example, they can afford to have training programs and they often have large brand name clients that you can come to interact with. However, I think it is important to prioritize some of these benefits. Is a ride home in a company car or a good dental plan more important than having meaningful and enjoyable work?

Some questions to ask yourself when choosing a career are: *What kind of future would I like to create for myself? What legacy would I like to leave behind? What do I want my obituary to say?* By thinking about and creating a strategy for the future, you will dramatically affect the quality of your attention and the choices you make in the present moment. All too often we forget to answer questions like these and narrowly focus on the short term. While short-term strategies can effectively accomplish short-term goals, they will not necessarily accomplish your long-term goals that are important to you, especially if you do not know what they are. As a result, we can end up short-changing ourselves by creating a life that we do not really want.

I started playing tennis tournaments when I was 14 years old. By the time I was 16 I had reached a respectable ranking in my area. However, my growth since then as a player has been much slower. When looking back, I can see that one of the reasons my game was held back was my limited strategy — which was to use my speed and consistency. In the short term, the strategy was effective and allowed me to win matches against most of the people in my area. However, it became less effective as I played better players, who would simply overpower me. No matter how well I played, their strategy easily defeated mine. Looking back, I can see that I failed to improve not because of my ability, but because of my strategy. My strategy helped me rise to middle-dom, but certainly not to stardom in the long term. Although it was more effective at first, it eventually hurt me. The chart below, which I introduced earlier in the book, illustrates the analogy more clearly. I followed the red path. Although I did very well in the beginning, in the long term I simply couldn't compete.

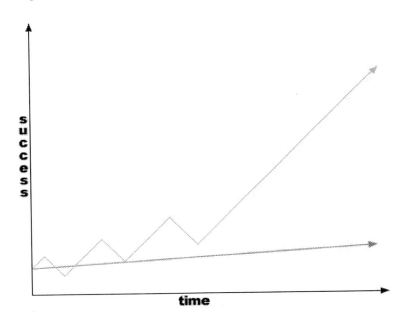

This analogy can be extended to the life you would like to create for yourself. According to research done for the National Foundation for Teaching

Entrepreneurship, "Most adolescents only project into the mid 20s." Take a moment to think again about the legacy you would like to leave behind. When you are on your deathbed and looking back on your life, what do you want to see? What strategy are you using now and what strategy do you want to be using throughout your career? How will the strategy you choose affect the tangible and intangible assets you invest in? The Extreme Entrepreneurship philosophy is based on what it takes to rise to stardom. If you are interested in creating long-term value, then you will be able to benefit from this philosophy.

The Power of Compound Interest and Assets

In the *Rich Dad, Poor Dad* series, Robert Kiyosaki provides a helpful way of looking at an asset. He compares it to an employee. An employee of a company creates value for the company owners. Similarly, an asset creates value for its owner. Therefore, the more you invest in assets, the more "employees" you will have working for you. With more employees, you will be able to add more value and accomplish your goals more quickly.

A unique part of an asset is that it creates more and more value over time. The following table illustrates this concept well:[8]

Part I: Extreme Entrepreneurship Defined

Age	Investor A Investment	Investor B Investment
18	$2,000	$0
19	2,000	0
20	2,000	0
21	2,000	0
22	2,000	0
23	2,000	0
24	0	2,000
25	0	2,000
…	0	2,000
59	0	2,000
Interest = 12%	Total Invested: $12,000	Total Invested: $70,000
	Total at age 60: $959,793	Total at age 60: $966,926

Although investor A invested $58,000 less than investor B, they both ended up with similar totals. Investor A's money was doing the work for him/her between ages 23 and 59, while investor B was continually putting in money until the age of 59.

You may be thinking to yourself: Compound interest sure sounds like a great idea, but I don't have an extra $2,000 every year. Furthermore, I don't want to wait until I'm 59 to use the money. But the above chart is just a sample of the power of having an asset work for you. There are *intangible* as well as tangible assets that you can invest in right now while enjoying yourself and investing very few resources.

Part II: Extreme Entrepreneurship Applied

The greatest acts of courage tend to be committed by entrepreneurs. I've never – I repeat, never – met anyone who has left his job, whether fired or voluntarily, who started his own business and regretted it. What these people always regret is not having done it sooner. That includes people who eventually went bust and had to go back to work for someone else.

— Harvey Mackay

4

Tangible & Intangible Assets

Tangible Assets

This section of the book talks about tangible assets and how to leverage them. If you are already familiar with tangible assets, such as real estate, stocks, and businesses you may want to skip to the next section of the book.

Creating your own business, buying stocks, or even buying real estate are relevant assets for students. Each asset has a certain level or risk attached to it, but at the same time provides students the opportunity to earn very high returns on their investment.

Starting a business is especially powerful because it can be done on a very low budget with little experience and still be very successful on a tangible and intangible level. For example, the startup costs of a web development company a friend and I started when we were in high school was $100. In fact, the median funding for the *Inc. 500* (http://www.inc.com/inc500) companies of 1999 was only $10,000.

Leveraging Other People's Tangible Assets

Entrepreneurs can get start-up funding though loans and/or equity investments. Both loans and equity investments cost you nothing to acquire.

Loans. With a loan you can borrow money at a certain interest rate (i.e., 8%) that you will have to pay back in the future and then invest it in your business that earns an even a higher interest rate (i.e., 20%). In other words, a $1,000 loan from a bank may allow you to buy an essential piece of equipment that will increase your company's profit by 20%. Thus, even though you had to pay the bank money to get the loan, you still were able to profit.

In 1997, David Bowie, the British rock star, issued "Bowie Bonds" backed by royalties from his albums. The $55-million issue of 10-year notes was bought in its entirety by Prudential Insurance Co. of America, at an interest rate of 7.9%. If he is able to leverage his brand name and musical talent in the right way, he can earn a lot more than the interest he has to pay.

Equity Investments. With equity investments, you give away a portion of your asset in return for funding to grow it larger. Three types of equity investments relevant to entrepreneurs are Initial Public Offerings (IPOs), venture capital and "angel" financing. IPOs are when a company sells shares of stock to the public. Venture capitalists (VCs) receive money from institutions and other sources that trust that the VC's contacts, knowledge, and business sense will provide them with a good return on their money. VCs typically invest hundreds of thousands and millions of dollars in companies to help them grow. Angel investors, on the other hand, are often family, friends, or wealthy individuals, and typically invest thousands to hundreds of thousands of dollars. The chart below illustrates how leveraging other people's tangible assets may decrease your ownership percentage, but increase the monetary size of your personal stake in the asset.

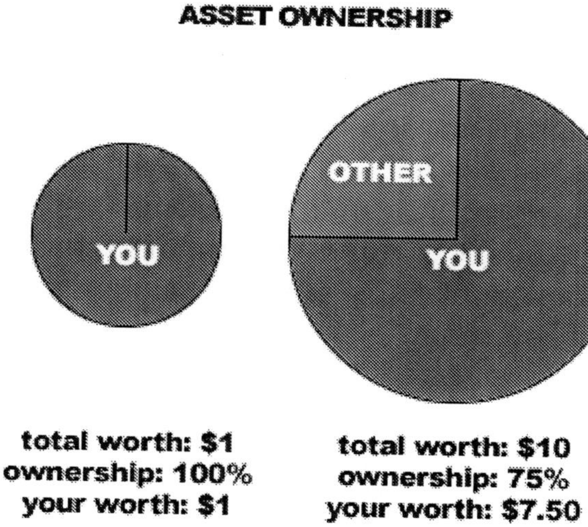

ASSET OWNERSHIP

total worth: $1
ownership: 100%
your worth: $1

total worth: $10
ownership: 75%
your worth: $7.50

Grants. Another way to leverage other people's tangible assets is through grants. Grants are a form of funding that you do not have to repay.

Leveraging Your Own Tangible Assets

As the paragraphs above illustrate, other people's tangible assets (loans, grants, and equity investments), are powerful methods of increasing your net worth.

However, leveraging other people's tangible assets can take a lot of time and or be very difficult. For example, getting a loan might be difficult because of bad credit or lack of collateral. Another option is to invest in your company with your own money. This may be a good idea if you do not need that much to get your company off the ground and it would take less time to work for the money you needed than to look for and apply to a loan, equity investment, or grant. Or, if you choose, there are many low-cost businesses you can start where you leverage your own financial assets.
"Bootstrapping" is a term used for people who finance a company's growth with its earnings and their own money. Many of the largest companies in the world were started in this fashion. In fact, "over 80% of *Inc. 500* (http://www.inc.com/inc500) founders bootstrapped their ventures with modest funds derived from credit cards, personal savings, second mortgages, and so on."

Intangible Assets

Intangible assets are those assets that can not be smelled, touched, seen, heard, or tasted. In my opinion, they are even more important and powerful than tangible ones. Intangible assets include your health, networking, branding, development, and growth, which are all very important and serve as a base for your tangible assets. Napoleon Hill, author of *Think and Grow Rich*, confirms this with the following statement: "The seed of every fortune is an idea." Without financial savvy, a skill, or other intangible qualities, an individual can not create a fortune. The same holds true for any other physical creation. The following excerpt from *The Master-Key to Riches* also by Hill, nicely illustrates the power of the intangible.

> *Man consists of two forces, one tangible, in the form of his physical body ... and the other intangible.*
>
> *Science teaches us the tangible portion of a man weighing one hundred and sixty pounds is composed of about seventeen chemical elements, all of which are known. They are:*
>
> | | |
> |---:|:---|
> | 95 | *pounds of oxygen* |
> | 38 | *pounds of carbon* |
> | 15 | *pounds of hydrogen* |
> | 4 | *pounds of nitrogen* |
> | 4.5 | *pounds of calcium* |
> | 6 | *ounces of chlorine* |
> | 4 | *ounces of sulfur* |
> | 3.5 | *ounces of potassium* |
> | 3 | *ounces of sodium* |
> | .25 | *ounces of iron* |
> | 2.5 | *ounces of fluorine* |
> | 2 | *ounces of magnesium* |
> | 1.5 | *ounces of silicon* |
> | | *Small traces of arsenic, iodine and aluminum* |
>
> *These tangible parts of man are worth only a few cents commercially and may be purchased in any modern chemical plant...Add to these chemical elements a well developed and properly organized and controlled ego, and they may be worth any price the*

owner sets upon them.

Intangible assets have four major unique qualities. These are:

1. They operate under the law of abundance. In other words, you can increase them by giving them away. With tangible items, you lose whatever you give away. A few examples:

    a. By showing love to a family member you not only transfer love to the other person, but you also create it inside of you.
    b. By giving away knowledge through teaching, you not only help others, but you learn the topic you're teaching even better.
    c. By introducing two people, or sharing a contact, you can create value for each individual as well as yourself because each will appreciate your action.

2. Nobody can ever take away your personal growth, development, or your health without your permission.

3. You can *always*, no matter where you are, invest in the intangible assets of personal growth, development, and health.

4. You cannot always change what you do, but you can always change *how* you do what you do. Our environment will have an effect on us, but

we have the ability to choose how we respond to it. Mother Theresa spent much of her time volunteering in distressed areas, yet she was able to rise above her environment with love and compassion. Victor Frankl, the author of *In Search of Meaning*, survived a few years in concentration camps. At one point he came to the realization that he possessed a mental freedom that nobody else could take away from him. By exercising his ability to make his own choices, he could have more freedom than those imprisoning him.

Benjamin Franklin once said, "If a man empties his purse into his head, no man can take it away from him. An investment in knowledge always pays the best interest." Not only can gathering knowledge and applying it to your life be extremely enjoyable, but your knowledge is constantly paying you back by influencing your decisions and actions. These decisions will in turn affect the quality and path of your life.

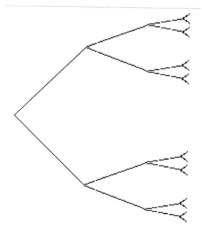

Consider the "decision tree" to the left, where each branch is a different decision. Making one decision differently can make a considerable difference in the long run. Therefore, when you gain knowledge that helps you make better decisions, you are changing the path your life follows. As time goes by, the benefit of making better decisions grows exponentially.

Leveraging Other People's Intangible Assets

Consider that one of the best ways to invest in your intangible assets is by leveraging the intangible assets of others. There are many people who have decades of experience investing in their own intangible assets and if approached in the right way are willing to share them. Some specific assets that can be leveraged are:

1. **Other People's Brand.** By associating with other people and organizations you can leverage their brands. What job or internship would most add to your brand? Which college? What references and testimonials would be most valuable? Which individuals in your network would most add to your brand? What clients would most add to your brand?

2. **Other People's Network.** Many people have relationships with other individuals that could be beneficial to you. What kind of people would you like to have in your own network? How can you reach these people through people in your existing network?

3. **Other People's Energy.** Mutually beneficial exchanges are one of the best ways to use other people's energy. What activities are most valuable to you? What activities are least valuable? Who can you delegate these lower-

value activities to? What do you have to give in return so that they benefit from the exchange as well? How else could you use other people's energy to help you achieve your goals? Mutually beneficial exchanges can bring both tangible and intangible assets. Some examples of mutually beneficial exchanges are found in friendships, networking contacts, and employees.

4. **Other People's Experiences.** There are millions of people who have a lifetime of successes and failures that you can apply to your own life. Instead of using trial and error, you can leverage other people's experiences through devices such as books, seminars, conferences, school, mentors, teachers, and so on. These allow you to learn in a very short time what took somebody else a whole lifetime. Furthermore, you can learn from their mistakes so that you do not make those same mistakes in the future.

5. **Other People's Growth.** There are many people who have empowering beliefs, values, ideas, and worldviews that could be beneficial to your own. The mistake that many people make is that they either accept or reject these without thinking things through. It is a very valuable and important skill to be able to differentiate between empowering and limiting worldviews and then expand and apply the empowering ones to your own life. There is nothing unoriginal about the process of "copying" or

building on other people's growth. If copying the right thing were so easy then we would be living a perfect world. To quote Albert Einstein, "All the valuable things, material, spiritual, and moral, which we receive from society can be traced back through countless generations to certain creative individuals."

What is your life vision and what are your goals? How do you need to grow to accomplish these? What resources could you leverage to accomplish this growth?

5

<u>Have Your Assets Do the Work</u>

Every Act Rewards Itself.
— Roy Emerson

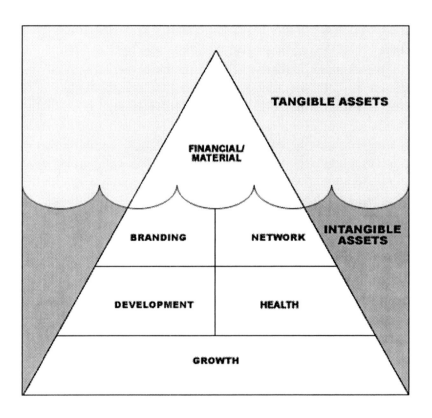

The above chart illustrates the assets I will focus on and how they relate to each other. Imagine the pyramid as an iceberg. Above water we can only see the tip of an iceberg, however, most of it is below the surface. The same is true for assets. We can see tangible assets, but not the larger base of intangible assets on which they rest.

Tangible assets are the tip of the iceberg and what people see and focus on. They are easy to see and measure. If I cut my hair, the change is immediately seen by others. Also, I can say that my hair is "x" inches shorter. Because tangible assets are easier to measure, they are often what people use to judge success, and thus seem more important.

Intangible assets are not easy to measure but have a very large impact on our happiness and success. Some examples of intangible assets are values, beliefs, knowledge, skills, attitude, relationships, and so on.

Blend, Don't Balance

A key point to keep in mind about intangible and tangible assets is *blend, don't balance*. A well-rounded person does not compartmentalize life and balance between different assets. He or she combines the different parts of life so that each activity and way of being complements the next and so it is possible to be invest in many assets 100% at the same time. For example, by investing your time and money in having better relationships, you not only improve your relationships outside of work, but you also improve your relationships at work. Thus, learning how to have better relationships can make you and the company you work with more profitable. Eating and sleeping well can not only improve your health, but also lead to you learning more and building a better brand because you are more pleasant to be around. Both of these benefits can lead to you achieving more at work.

Blending is done by creating or finding activities and ways of being where you can invest in more than one asset at a time. For example, by starting your own business, you can develop credentials, meet new contacts, learn, grow, and eventually amass a great fortune. By starting a business with an empowering mindset, you might increase your success, as well as your enjoyment and fulfillment.

Many people separate work and enjoyment. Furthermore, many people equate enjoyment and living life to its fullest with investing in liabilities instead of assets. As such, many people reward their hard work with eating or drinking poorly or making decisions that are detrimental. An Extreme Entrepreneur, on the other hand, asks, "How can I work (invest in my assets) while enjoying myself?" He or she may search for food that tastes great and is healthy. Or socially, he or she may have fun without partying on the weekends or drinking a lot of alcohol. Living life to its fullest can mean enjoying the present moment *and* investing your assets.

6

The Six Core Assets

1. Financial (material)
Financial assets provide you with passive income, money you do not have to work for directly. In other words, financial assets can put money in your pocket while you are asleep. Examples of financial assets include stocks, bonds, real estate, or your own business.

2. Networking (a.k.a., team building)
By increasing the breadth and depth of your network, you increase your sphere of influence. The larger your sphere of influence the more decisions you will be able to affect. As a result, your chances of success will be increased. Your network includes relationships such as family, friends, acquaintances, and contacts. Your network is an extremely important asset and in the best of worlds can help you by:

- Building your brand by people in your network putting in a good word for you.
- Getting you introduced to people who can make decisions that benefit you. These may be potential employers, clients, and so on.
- Helping you to invest in your personal growth and personal development assets.

- Giving you support.
- Getting you a job or contract.
- Getting you an invitation and/or discount to an event.

You have probably heard phrases like, "Your network increases your net worth," or "It's not what you know, but who you know." Both phrases illustrate the power and potential of a strong network.

According to the "Six Degrees of Separation" theory, you are connected to anyone in the world through six relationships. You have probably already met thousands of people. Those people have met thousands and so on. With a quality, diverse network, you will expand your sphere of influence and be able to achieve your goals more quickly and easily. The image below illustrates how a network can grow exponentially:

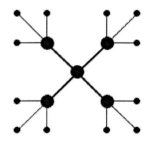

A network is an asset because it can grow and increase in quality without your involvement. For example, if you have a contact and he or she meets somebody new or learns a piece of information that can be valuable, value has been added to your network. The more people you have in your network the more value potentially exists.

3. Development

Your personal development can be broadly defined as your knowledge, habits, and skills. Brian Tracy, the author of *Focal Point*, says, "Almost everything you do is determined by your habits. I would venture at least 95 percent." While *we all have the ability to act any way we want to in any environment*, it can be difficult to do what you want if you have developed bad habits. For example, in close relationships people often fall into bad habits, and before long the relationship is ruined. However, we have great potential to accomplish our goals if we use habits to our advantage. Imagine the possibilities if your body was constantly pushing you to invest in your tangible and intangible assets with little effort on your part!

The "learning ladder" below is the process we use to acquire empowering knowledge, assimilate it into our lives as knowledge or a skill, and make it a habit.

Unconscious Incompetence. At first, we don't know what we don't know. Einstein once said, "I want to know God's thoughts... the rest are details." He had a strong desire to learn more about what he didn't already know. Before you picked up this book, you probably did not know what the "Extreme Entrepreneurship" philosophy was all about. In other words, you were unaware that you did not know about it. The goal of this book is to expand the reader's reality and bring him or her to "conscious incompetence. "

Conscious Incompetence. This represents that which you *know* you don't know. For example, you may be aware that taxes exist, but have no idea how to file your tax return.

Conscious Competence. This represents knowledge or skills that you know about and are competent in. For example, when you are first getting your driver's license, you know how to drive, but you still have to think about shifting gears, turning on your direction signals, and so on.

Unconscious Competence. Unconscious competence exists when knowledge or a skill is mastered and turns into a habit. It takes at least a few months to master driving. After awhile, you can start to have conversations or fiddle with the radio, and still drive very well. Sometimes the process gets so unconscious that you lose track of time and realize that you have all of a sudden reached your targeted destination.

According to one of psychology's most fundamental laws, the Law of Effect, everything we do reinforces itself. Therefore, as creatures of habit, it is important to cultivate positive habits. *Every decision is an opportunity to invest in an empowering habit.* As Horace Mann once said, "Habit is a cable; we weave a thread of it every day, and at last we cannot break it."

An example of where my habits used to work against me was in public speaking. I could logically think of many reasons why I should not be nervous and shaking, but that didn't help. On the other hand, your body's habits can work for you. For example, the Extreme Entrepreneurship philosophy is now ingrained in me to the point where I am motivated by the thought of investing in my tangible and intangible assets. I can spend an entire day writing, reading, or working on my business and be so passionate about it that I forget to eat.

The knowledge mastery process is extremely important to self-development. If one step of the process is not fully developed, it can create a "traffic jam" and have major negative impacts on a person's life. For example, if someone does not move from unconscious incompetence to conscious incompetence, the individual will reach a wall once he/she masters what is already known.

It takes a combination of openness and quality-filtration to bring the right amount and quality of knowledge into your awareness. It takes courage and proactiveness to turn an element of knowledge into a skill. Finally, it takes commitment to practice that skill until it becomes fully integrated into your life.

Expanding your comfort zone is crucial to having your emotions work with you. After you have done something once, it is much easier to do it again. However, the more you stay in the enclosed area where you feel comfortable the harder it will be to expand in the future. *Being comfortable being uncomfortable is crucial to leveraging your emotions.* Even though I have done much public speaking and improved a great deal, I still get a little nervous when I speak. Yet because I am comfortable doing it, I am constantly improving and creating new opportunities.

4. Personal Branding

How you brand yourself is critical. Consider Coca-Cola. Their physical assets amount to only $8 billion. On the other hand, their brand is one of the most recognizable in the world and is worth around $80 billion. Or consider the Virgin name. By leveraging the Virgin brand name, Richard Branson has been able to branch off into the soft drink, financial service, telecom, and airline industries and create hundreds of millions of dollars in wealth. In the same way that companies have a brand, individuals have one. By becoming aware that you *are* a brand, you too can leverage it to achieve your goals.

The personal brand as I define it has three parts:

    a. Communication — what you say about yourself (words, body language, voice).
    b. Credentials — what "paper" says about you.
    c. Reputation — what others say about you.

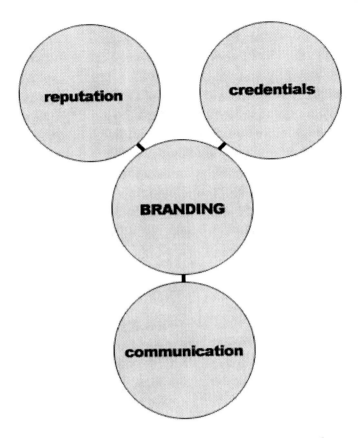

To have a powerful brand it is important to have the three parts working together to communicate the same message. As an asset, your brand can be leveraged to help you achieve your goals. For example, if you consistently go the extra mile and/or make a point of being honest, these positive characteristics may spread among people via word-of-mouth and become part of your brand. If your brand is strong enough other people will begin to spread your branding messages for you.

Try getting feedback from your network on what impressions people have of you. What do they think your strengths and weaknesses are? What do you need to change?

5. Health

Your health is a key intangible asset. If you do not eat, sleep, and exercise properly your body will be working against you instead of with you. The less attentive or the worse mood you are in, the higher probability you have of putting your valuable time into liabilities instead of assets. If you liken yourself to a computer, than your knowledge and growth would be the software and your body would be the hardware. The healthier your body is, the more effectively the software will run.

6. Growth

Growth is the core intangible asset. It can be broadly defined as your worldview. It includes your values, beliefs, attitude, and the paradigms from which you interpret life. It is the framework for your life.

Your personal growth is your core asset and therefore has the most leverage. Making a small investment in your growth can lead to extremely large dividends over time in both personal growth and your other assets. People who have been considered spiritual gurus have invested heavily in this asset.

Take a moment a look around you. What are you seeing, thinking, hearing, smelling, tasting, and touching? Now, imagine that you are a photographer.

What do you notice? What about an electrician, an interior designer, or an entrepreneur? With each different worldview comes different perceptions, each leading to a different end. This is why it is important to take control of your worldview and consciously evolve it.

The picture below is the framework of a building. Your personal growth serves as the framework of your life. If a building has a poor framework, then each brick makes the framework weaker until it ultimately collapses. With a strong framework, each new brick makes the building more durable. In the same way, a poor foundation in personal growth means that new experiences lead to liabilities. And liabilities lead to a larger downfall. We can see evidence of this now with the multitude of corporate scandals being uncovered. On the other hand, a strong foundation means that new experiences lead to more assets.

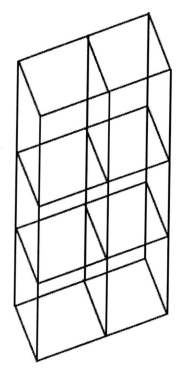

Building your life's framework is not a one-time deal. Growth is a process by which you constantly build and rebuild your foundation so that experiences in your life lead to more assets. Because growth is a process, you can never build a perfect framework. They are always going to have liabilities. Your job is to constantly find these liabilities and turn them into assets.

For example, a child might see that being selfish is beneficial. Therefore, the child might think that he or she is building a better framework by being selfish. While this may work at first, the child's friends might start to play with other kids and say unkind things about the child. As a result, the child in question might shift and start being overly gracious by giving away a lot of food, toys, and time to others. While this may make more friends, it will also result in going hungry at times and not having toys to play with. After these two extremes, the child might decide to be "self-interested." As such, the child might realize it is in his or her interest to eat enough food to be full and then give away the rest of it. This example, illustrates how a framework can grow and change over time by learning from experience.

Part III:
Extreme
Entrepreneurship
Model

Your life is the sum result of all the choices you make, both consciously and unconsciously. If you can control the process of choosing, you can take control of all aspects of your life. You can find the freedom that comes from being in charge of yourself.

— **Senator Robert. F. Bennett**

7

Extreme Entrepreneur
Model Overview

The Extreme Entrepreneur model brings together the main points of this book into a practical and useable form that can be easily applied to your life.

The thread that binds this model is *choice*. The ability to consciously make our own decisions is uniquely human. The power of conscious choice creates people like Martin Luther King and Gandhi, who rise above a limiting environment and make choices based on their values, beliefs, and vision.

Earlier in the book, I introduced the following model:

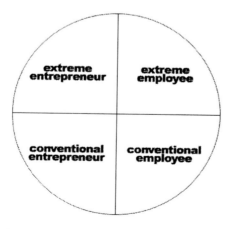

Part III: Extreme Entrepreneurship Model

This quadrant illustrates the four major choices we are always confronted with, whether we realize it or not:

1. **Extreme Entrepreneur** — choosing our reaction and our activities.

2. **Extreme Employee** — choosing our reaction within a limiting activity.

3. **Conventional Entrepreneur** — choosing our activity, but not our reaction.

4. **Conventional Employee** — Not choosing our activity or our reaction to it.

In each and every one of our waking moments, we are given the freedom to choose our activities and/or our reactions, regardless of our past choices. For every decision we make there is a consequence, as per the table below.

	Investment	Value
Extreme Entrepreneur	Assets	Add
Extreme Employee	Assets & Liabilities	Add & Subtract
Conventional Entrepreneur	Assets & Liabilities	Add & Subtract
Conventional Employee	Liabilities	Subtract

Financially, we can attract assets that put money back in our pockets while we sleep, or we can attract liabilities that take money out of our pockets while we sleep. The same concept holds true for brand, network, body, development, and growth. The chart below illustrates the asset/liability concept visually:

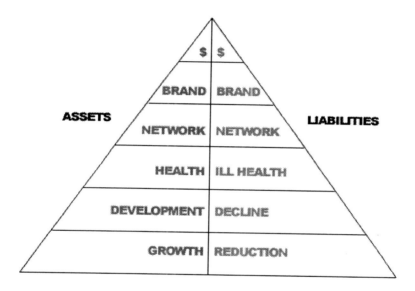

8

Decision Characteristics

To better understand the decisions we make, we must also look at the three core characteristics that affect them. These are:

1. Available Choices
2. Quality of Attention
3. Decision Power

Available Choices: At any given moment we have many choices available. What is available is, in large part, determined by choices we made in the past. When we are able to consistently make positive decisions, we not only improve our ability to make the best decision available, but also widen our available choices.

Quality of Attention: By being more aware of our internal and external environments, we have more information from which to make decisions. With increased awareness and growth comes the ability to detach ourselves from the heat of the situation when necessary and consider all our decisions. For example, when you are in the heat of an argument with somebody you may be so unaware of yourself and surroundings that you do not realize that what you are saying is ridiculous, harmful to you, or not helping you reach the outcome you would like. Sometimes our awareness is so low that we may let a silly argument in the morning ruin our entire day.

Decision Power: Decision power is the ability to be aware of the best decision available *and* to make it. Oftentimes, we are aware of our best decision but make a poor choice anyway and then rationalize it. Not only will you have to deal with the consequences of making a poor choice, but you will be forming a habit of rationalizing poor decisions.

A great example of people exerting poor decision power is with the food they eat. People (including myself) eat what they know is bad for them and then rationalize the decision by claiming:

- They are too young to pay the consequences of what they eat.
- They want to live life to the fullest by eating the best-tasting foods.

A person with a broader awareness and better decision power might see that there are many foods that taste great and are healthy too. Living life to its fullest does not necessarily mean going out every Friday or Saturday night. It can also mean enjoying every day of the week and investing in your future with every decision.

9

Ramifications of Our Choices

The assets and/or liabilities we invest in now
determine the choices we have available and the
choices we make in the future. If we choose to eat
poorly, we may be more irritable. Being irritable may
result in making choices we regret, such as getting in
unnecessary arguments. This could result in more
liabilities by weakening our network. The illustration
below illustrates how all the decisions we make in the
present are connected to those in the future:

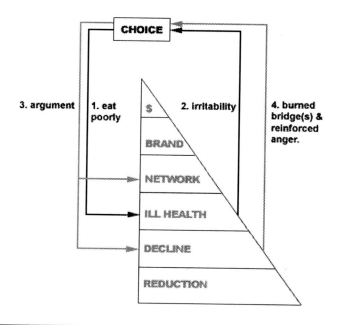

The illustration above is an example of a "negative feedback loop." This occurs when we continually makes choices that invest in our liabilities. With each negative choice, it becomes easier to make another negative choice and more difficult to make a positive one. In the illustration above, the person eats poorly. This might mean too much sugar. As a result, they have an energy high, but they quickly plummet in energy and become irritable. As a result of being irritable, the individual gets in an argument over something silly and damages a relationship.

The same principle holds true for **positive feedback loops**. With each positive choice we make, it becomes easier to make another one. For example, if you make a great contact and build a lasting relationship, you will then have access to improved branding (i.e., letter of recommendation, name dropping), growth, and more like-minded contacts.

In these ways the decisions we make now affect our current assets and/or liabilities, as well as our future choices. Thus, each choice you make in the present has hidden benefits/costs in the future.

Now we can begin to understand the belief that all humans are capable of great good and great evil. The only difference between pursuing good or evil are the choices (no matter how seemingly large or small) we make in the present moment and what feedback loop we choose to follow.

Feedback from an asset or liability affects the choices we have, the choices we see, and the choices we take. For example:

- A poor reputation may give us fewer career choices because employers will not to employ somebody with a bad reputation.

- Poor growth may make us aware of fewer options. We always have the ability to be motivated, loving, or caring. However, we are not always aware of this. Sometimes we forget when we are arguing with a loved one that being caring or loving is even an option. A person with a high level of growth will be aware of the highest-value options available.

- Poor development may make it very difficult to make the right choice. For example, have you ever known that you were making a bad choice and done it anyway? Have you ever eaten poorly even though you knew it was not good for you? While being aware of the best decision is important, it means nothing if you cannot choose to follow it.

Now that you have a clear understanding of how important choices are, I will give you a model that will help you process what I have said thus far. The following four charts represent not only the short-term effects of our decisions, but the long term as well. Through the awareness of the long-term effects of our decisions, we are more capable of making decisions that are beneficial in both the short and long term, as opposed to only one or the other. When making decisions in the present, think about where you want to be in the future. What does your ideal world look like? If your current decisions are taking you away from this ideal, you may want to reconsider them.

The charts below also illustrate that decisions do not come every once in awhile. We are confronted with decisions every moment. Every decision we make, no matter how small it seems, is part of a process that can have large, long-term effects on our life.

Extreme Entrepreneur: We make the choice to be an Extreme Entrepreneur by choosing an empowering activity and way of being. By making this choice we invest in our tangible and intangible assets and make it easier to be an Extreme Entrepreneur in the future.

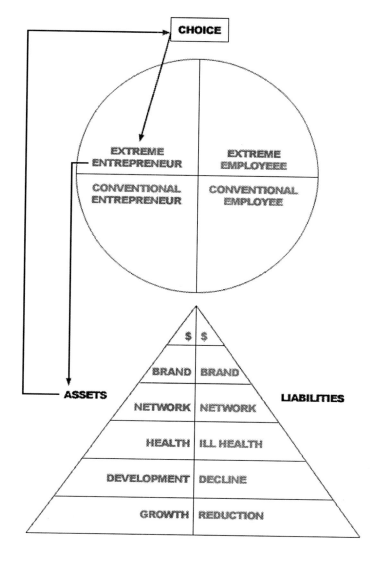

Conventional Entrepreneur: We make the choice to be a conventional entrepreneur by choosing to follow the conventional way of being in an empowering activity. An example is someone who goes to Harvard, but constantly cheats and chooses a major because everybody else is going into that field. As you can see, the person still invests in his or her assets, but also invests in his or her liabilities.

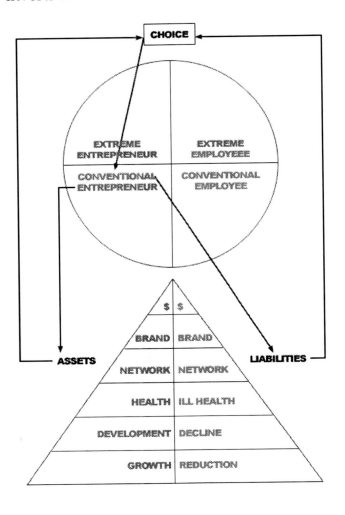

Extreme Employee: The extreme employee chooses the limiting activity but acts in an empowering way. An example of this is an individual who runs an illegal business. No matter how well the person runs the business, he or she still runs the risk of being arrested and put in jail, or killed.

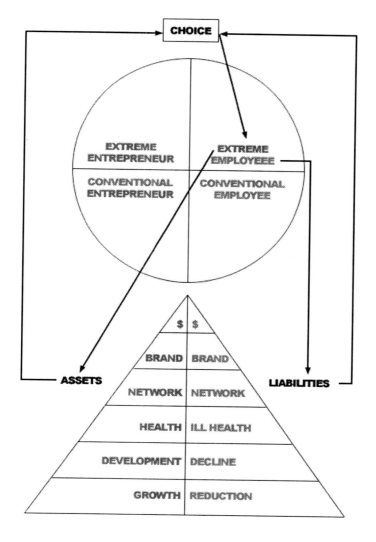

Conventional Employee: We make the choice to be a conventional employee by choosing to follow limiting ways of being in limiting activities. An example of this is an individual who poorly runs an illegal business and hates doing it. This results in a spiraling down as a result of making poor choices.

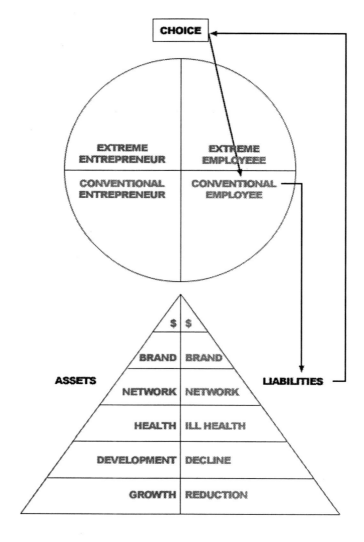

Now that you have an understanding of the ramifications of your choices, you should be able to make better ones. It is now up to you to commit to being an Extreme Entrepreneur. You need to ask yourself how important it is to you. If you were an Extreme Entrepreneur, what would you have to do differently? What would you have to start doing? How might your life be improved in 5 years? 10 years? 20 years?

Part IV:
The Extreme Endeavor Curriculum

Most people live and die with their music unplayed. They never dare to try.

– Mary Kay Ash, founder, Mary Kay Cosmetics

10

Self-Education

*Self-education is, I firmly believe, the
only kind of education there is.*
— Isaac Asimov, author

Our brain grows most rapidly, and we learn the most,
during early childhood. Miraculously, we are able to
do so without going to school or setting aside time for
formal learning. We follow our natural curiosity as we
happily engage in life!

Unfortunately, when we enter school, most of us end
up doing work that we do not enjoy. Learning often
becomes tedious and "uncool." In fact, being able to get
high scores without studying becomes admirable. As a
result, learning or doing work on our own becomes
undesirable. While some people are able to relearn
their passion for learning and growth, many do not. In
fact, I once read a statistic that said the average adult
only reads two books over their lifetime after they
finish school. I do not know if this statistic is true, but I
think it is safe to say that many individuals stop
prioritizing learning once they graduate from school.

However, to succeed in today's quickly evolving
society we really need to be able to enjoy learning and
incorporate it into our everyday life in and out of

school. This quote from Henry Thoreau summarizes the concept: "How could youth better learn to live than by at once trying the experiment of living?"

With the research I have done on people who are successful in their fields, I have never met anybody who has not created their own learning curriculum to go above and beyond what they were taught in school. To be in the small minority of Extreme Entrepreneurs, self-education is a necessity. The challenge of Extreme Entrepreneurship is for individuals to create their own self-education curriculum that transcends school/non-school lines and integrates into all areas of life. Creating your own curriculum means:

- Creating your own lesson plans (so to speak).
- Creating your own measures of success.
- Creating your own goals.
- Committing your life to self-education.
- Learning more about how you learn best.

Creating your own curriculum should not be boring but inspiring. As poet William Butler Yeats once said, "Education is not the filling of a pail, but the lighting of a fire."

In this part of the book, I share inspiring projects that I or other students have undertaken and talk about how you can create a self-education curriculum that works for you. In addition, I will give my advice on how to make your curriculum compatible with your school's (if you are in school).

11

Extreme Endeavor Overview

Be nobody but yourself in a world which is doing its best - night and day - to make you everybody else.
— E.E. Cummings, poet

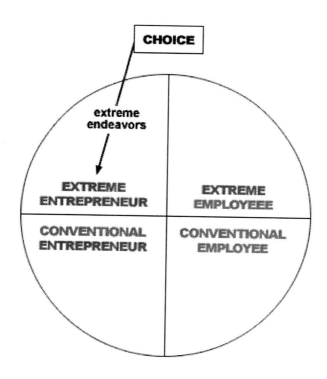

An Extreme Endeavor is any activity that applies the extreme mindset within an empowering activity (framework). For example, an extreme endeavor might be passionately and persistently starting and operating a business. Starting your own business is an empowering activity because it allows you to invest in your assets in many ways. It is through Extreme Endeavors that we become Extreme Entrepreneurs. This is how we invest in our tangible/intangible assets and encourage a positive feedback loop.

Setting Goals

The pursuit of a goal brings order in awareness because a person must concentrate attention on the task at hand and momentarily forget everything else. These periods of struggling to overcome challenges are what people find to be the most enjoyable times of their lives.
    – Mihaly Csikszentmihalyi, author of *Flow*

Extreme Endeavors are particularly powerful ways for giving and receiving value. However, to know what is of "value" to you, you must create your own goals. Goals are outcomes you would like to achieve. Goal setting is the process of finding and pursuing what is of value to you.

If you do not know clearly what you want and how you are going to get there, you will be more susceptible to what others consciously or unconsciously want you to do or be. The clearer you make your own goals and vision, the less likely it will be that you can be deterred from your path. As the saying goes, "If you don't know where you are going, then any road will take you there."

Chapter 11: Extreme Endeavor Overview

Assuming the majority is right and just following along can be a major risk. While the majority might be correct, there are many times when it is not. Following the majority at these times could cost you some of the best opportunities of your life. A few months ago, I was in a long line with a throng of people waiting to go up one staircase. There was an empty staircase right next to the one full of people. My first assumption was that it must have been off limits, but immediately following that I thought to myself, "Oh what the hell, why don't I just try it? What is the worst that can happen?" When I ventured up the empty staircase unimpeded, I realized that the only reason people had not been taking it was that nobody else was. Then upon looking back, I realized that there were actually people following me up, thus confirming my conclusion. My question is, do you want to take the unused staircase and make a path for others to follow, or do you want to push and shove with the majority just to get up the staircase everybody else is already on?

In many ways you can see the evolution of a person's growth by looking at what they want to achieve. Goals usually reflect people's beliefs and values and, more generally, their personal growth. In the Extreme Endeavor model, goals can be created for all of your assets. In the case of development and growth, you must not only consider what you want to do, but how you are going to do it. Some examples of goals are:

Money: To have $5,000 (living expenses for six months saved by "x" date).

Branding: To win next year's "Extreme Entrepreneur of the Year Award."

Networking: To shadow the CEO of ABC.com for one week next summer.

Body: To drink eight glasses of water every day.

Development: To improve my writing so that I can publish an article in the school newspaper.

Growth: To create a list of 20 values that I would like to bring into my life, create a poster with them, and post them around my house by next week.

Characteristics of Goals

1. **Goals Transform Your Present-Moment and Give it Direction and Inspiration.** By taking the time to think about what you want in the future you will learn more about yourself and what is important to you. As a result, you will begin to realize the new path you must take and new ways you must be and act to achieve your goals. So, even though your goals will change, you will still have spent time going down a path that excites and inspires you.

2. **Goal Setting Is a Process, Not an End.** In the same way goals for a business change, as new information arises, so it should be in your personal life. By setting and pursuing goals, you are reflecting on what is important to you. There is a high probability that, as you pursue a goal, you will realize it is wrong for you. This will be a profound realization that is part of the process. In fact, without pursuing the goal you may not have realized that having "x" number of dollars and "y" number of friends wasn't important to you. By realizing what is *not* important, you can concentrate on the goals that are worthy of your pursuit. You cannot fool anybody. If you choose a goal just because you think you should, then you will not be inspired.

3. **Goals Should Be Ends As Well As Processes.** In other words, you should plan where you want to go and how you want to get there. For example, an end goal could be earning a million dollars before the age of 30. A process goal could be maximizing your love for yourself and others so you don't consistently get angry at the people closest to you.

4. **Goals Should Be Specific and Clear.** It is easy to simply say: "I want a lot of money." This may be a good starting point. However, as you think more about what is important to you, the goal should become more specific. What is "a lot of money"? Is it $100,000 or $1 billion? Why do you want it? When do you want to achieve it by?

When you are 30? Or 60? Each end will require different means. Furthermore, each end will require different actions in the present-moment, and therefore different paths.

5. **Goals Should Be Magic in the Long Run.** There is something powerful in creating long-term goals that seem as if magic would be the only way to achieve them. Christopher Columbus had the magical goal of sailing around a world that others believed was flat. The Wright brothers believed they could create a machine that would fly in the air, around the time the first car was being invented. The whole way your mind thinks is transformed by magical goals and you become inspired. Although you may not believe you can achieve the goal at first, the process of achieving it might get you somewhere in between. Falling short of $1 million by $100,000 is not too shabby.

Choosing a goal that you greatly desire and that you are willing to work hard enough to achieve is crucial. You do not want a goal that is so unchallenging that you become bored. Some people make the mistake of classifying themselves as "unmotivated." However, everybody has the potential to be motivated. Have you ever been really hungry for a specific food and determined to get it? Have you ever been really afraid of something and motivated to avoid it? Everyone at some point or other has been extremely motivated either towards or away from something. Both positive and negative motivation can be effective depending on the individual. A key to Extreme Entrepreneurship is consciously choosing what you want to go after in life and avoiding what you do not want.

A goal should not be something that would just be nice to achieve. If a goal is only "logical" or "nice," than you will not have the fire power to pursue it when times are tough and you need inspiration the most. For your goals to be effective, you will have to realize its importance at your core and be emotionally stirred. The more emotion you involve, the better. What are your worst habits, the ones you cannot seem to shake? Take a second to imagine how much opportunity you would lose if you kept this habit for the next year, ten years, twenty years, or the rest of your life. How would these habits negatively affect your money, brand, network, health, development, and growth over time? Is this acceptable to you? If it is not acceptable to you, what are you going to do? What compelling goals are you going to create?

6. **Goals Should Be Measurable.** If you cannot measure your goals, you cannot measure how effective your current plan is. And if you cannot measure how effective your current plan is, you cannot make corrective measures. As a result, you will both stagnate and fit the following definition of insane, "An individual who keeps

on doing the same thing expecting different results."

7. **Goals Should Blend with Each Other.** Another important part of goal setting is establishing relations between your goals. By blending your goals, you will make it possible to work on more than one at a time. For example, in a marketing research class I took, I was able to do the major market research project on my business. Thus I was essentially able to work on my business and school goals at the same time.

How can you connect your goals so that achieving one helps achieve another? The answer is a "goal hierarchy" (see example below). This will give you the big picture of all your short-term and long-term goals in areas such as money, brand, network, health, development, and growth. With this long-term view you can get a better picture of how your goals are working together to create your life plan.

To create a goal hierarchy, you first have to take time to create a vision for your life, which will go in the center of the chart. Your life vision is very likely to change over time. However, by going through the process of deciding what your vision is, creating a plan to achieve it, and then taking action on your plan, you can see if the vision is right for you.

After you realize what your life vision is, you can create supporting goals to help accomplish them. From these supporting goals, will develop others, until finally you will come down to specific tasks that you can do right now. The chart below is an example of a hierarchy in the form of a "mind map" and is an easy way to create your goals and link them together. The chart only shows two levels of the mind map. If you were to continue, then each goal would be broken down into the specific steps needed to achieve it.

12

The Extreme Endeavors

*I had not lived there a week before my feet wore a path·from
my door to the pond-side; and through it is five or six years
since I trod it, it is still quite distinct. It is true, I fear, that
others may have fallen into it, and so helped to keep it open.
The surface of the earth is soft and impressible by the feet of
man; and so with the paths which the mind travels. How
worn and dusty, then, must be the highways of the world,
how deep the ruts of tradition and conformity.*
— Henry David Thoreau, author

While taking a semester off from New York University,
I created my own learning curriculum in more detail
than I ever had before. Now that I am back at NYU, I
still have my own curriculum, which I've blended with
NYU's curriculum.

I recently overheard an interesting conversation in an
NYU computer lab. A student was talking about her
aggravation about a job interview she had just had. The
interviewer asked her what she liked doing. Her first
response was to talk about the tasks she would like to
perform while working at the company. The
interviewer interrupted her and said, "No, I mean what
do you like to do besides school. What are your
interests and hobbies? For example, I like traveling and
writing." Taken aback, the student paused, and then

said that she did not really have time to develop hobbies since she was so busy with school. By the way the student was talking, I could tell that she thought the interviewer was not understanding of how hard school was and how hard she needed to work at it.

This example illustrates an interesting phenomenon. Many students are willing to do something for many years they do not enjoy and are not passionate about. The interesting thing is that all the research I have done points to the fact that you must be passionate about what you do to be successful at it in the long run.

To be successful on a tangible and intangible level you must follow your heart and in so doing break away from the mainstream. By breaking away from the mainstream you become a big fish in your own pond instead of a small fish in a big pond. Instead of breaking away from the pack and being passionate later, why not start earlier? Why not start being passionate and following your heart right now? Breaking away will only be more difficult as you get older!

The Extreme Endeavors I have listed below are only examples to consider as you create your own curriculum. They are endeavors that I have found to be particularly fruitful. One or more the endeavors will be a great way for you to begin your journey of finding your passion and prioritizing what is most important to you.

The fifteen endeavors I will focus on are:

1. Starting and Running a Business
2. Scholarships/Awards/Competitions
3. Shadowing
4. Seminars/Conferences/Organization and Association Meetings
5. Strategic Volunteering
6. Mastermind/Junto/Salon
7. Informational Interviews/Mentors
8. Journaling
9. "Vuja Daze"
10. Investing in Real Estate to Live in
11. Saving Money
12. Investing Money
13. Taking Time Off
14. Leveraging School
15. Jobs and Internships

Starting and Running a Business

Description

Starting and running a business at its simplest level involves registering your company, coming up with a product/service, and marketing it. Entrepreneurship experience is extremely valuable when you are a student because you can follow your passion, make a lot of money, make a difference, and improve your intangible assets, all at the same time.

Benefits:

1. **You gain experience.** Owning and operating your own business is an incredible way to gain experience and credentials, regardless of whether you decide to stay in business once you graduate. Jaime Gonzalez, of Oklahoma State University, received the highest job offer in his entire graduating class. However, there are two kickers. First, he had a 2.4 GPA. Second, he was the founder of an IT consulting company. I think it's a pretty fair guess that his student entrepreneurship experience had something to do with it.

2. **You have nothing to lose.** I think it is safe to say that most students dip into their parents' checkbook when it comes time to pay the bills. In general, students do not pay child support, rent, utilities and many other expenses. The worst thing that could happen if your business

fails is that you will get a job, have an impressive credential on your resume, and have experiences that will increase your chances of success in the future. Starting a business can still be beneficial if it fails because going through the process shows employers that you have gained experience and that you learned on your own buck rather than on theirs. The best thing that can happen is that you will create the next Microsoft. I don't know about you, but I think that is better than choosing between no job and a job that you're in just for the money.

3. **Two-thirds of millionaires are entrepreneurs,** according to Thomas Stanley and William Dank, authors of _The Millionaire Mind_. If it is money you want, then consider entrepreneurship. You will not only receive a salary, but also a _lot_ of money if you are lucky enough to sell your company or take it public. Michael Furdyk, a successful young entrepreneur, was able to sell his business, MyDesktop.com, for $1 million when he was 16 years old!

4. **You develop a network.** You have likely heard that your network increases your net worth. Consider the fact that, by running a business and being in a business community, you will develop excellent contacts. If you choose to get a job after you graduate, you will have a great pool of people who will be more than happy to hire you or send your resume to somebody who will want to. Joshua Newman, a serial

entrepreneur, was hired by his former client, the Gerson Lehrman Group, as a senior technology analyst after graduating from Yale.

5. **You increase your value.** Put simply, starting a business in college increases the value of your brand and gives you more options. For example, an entrepreneur with a noticeable brand value can publish a book, star in a documentary movie (i.e., Startup.com), or go straight to the top of another company. I recently met one of the founders of Diversity Planet, a job-search web site for minorities. He spent a year working very hard on the company and has since left to take a reporting job with *Dateline NBC* at the ripe old age of 20! People often do not get an opportunity like that until they are much older.

6. **Operating a profitable business is less risky than being an employee in the long term.** For example, just look at the recent economic downturn. Tens of thousands of people have been laid off. The owners of profitable businesses are probably still with the businesses. They will be the last people to go down with a ship unless they are asked to step down because of poor performance. Business owners can have multiple streams of income from different customers. If you are an employee, you only have one stream of income from your employer and therefore are bearing more risk.

7. **Operating a profitable business can be less time-consuming than being an employee in the long term.** As an employee, you are a part of a system. Generally, as you gain more perks and benefits, you gain more responsibilities. As an entrepreneur, you create a system. As the company grows you can remove yourself from the system and still profit by selling shares of the company or receiving dividends. In other words, the entrepreneur gets paid more than once for each unit of work, while the employee only gets paid once.

8. **You will gain knowledge they do not teach in school.** Entrepreneurship is a combination of all the disciplines of business. Some of the fields it includes are marketing, accounting, management and operations. Business classes are often rooted in theory. Already having knowledge of these topics before you take the classes allows you to see more clearly how the theories apply practically. Also, you will be able to learn early on what subjects you like so you can make better decisions when choosing a major and deciding which industries to go into.

9. **It is yours.** You make the rules, create your own hours, work from wherever you want and choose who you want to work with. You can also pick what interests you the most in the world and then start a business that is related to that. If you like art, you can start a design business. If you like marketing, you can create

or choose a product and then market it. If you like writing, you can write a book and do your own public relations and marketing. If you like the Internet, you can start a Web-development business.

10. **You will grow and learn more about yourself.** I personally have grown a great deal from owning a business. As I mentioned earlier, I conquered my fear of public speaking. In addition, I had probably read a total of five books outside of school (and I read them because my mother urged me to). Since starting my business, I have probably read more than a hundred. The business has also allowed me to learn more about myself. I know that I will be an entrepreneur forever in some way, shape or form!

11. **The government helps entrepreneurs.** When you are an employee, your income is taxed. When you own a company, its profits (income minus expenses) are taxed. Businesses get tax deductions on items like computers, phones, home office space, mileage, and food related to the business.

People can create businesses as a completely separate entity from themselves by incorporating. It is possible that somebody could start a business, borrow a million dollars, eventually go bankrupt, and not be affected financially on a personal level.

In the United States, when individuals go bankrupt, they are able to get back on their feet. In other countries, people lose credibility and can be jailed for going bankrupt. It makes sense to take advantage of the opportunities that the government gives to business owners by becoming one yourself.

12. Make a difference. "Sixty-seven percent of inventions and ninety-five percent of all radical innovations since World War II are attributable to small entrepreneurs. Most of the new jobs created in this country in the past decade have been created by small, not big, businesses… Presently, almost half of all new products are created by small, entrepreneurial companies."[9] "Almost half of the workforce in the United States is employed by small businesses."[8] "Most foundations throughout the country with major leadership roles in philanthropy were initially endowed by entrepreneurs who had amassed wealth through the success of the entrepreneurial ventures they had conceived and initiated…The history of philanthropy in the US shows most large charitable foundations were started with significant endowments by successful entrepreneurs. Andrew Carnegie, Henry Ford, John D. Rockefeller, W.W. Kellogg, J. Howard Pew, Alfred P. Sloan, Charles Stewart Mott, and Ewing Marion Kauffman are but a few who have earning this distinction."[10]

13. **Your business can help school and vice-versa.** I recently took a summer marketing course and the main project for the class was to write a marketing plan. The teacher allowed me to write a plan for my own business, thus allowing me to kill two birds with one stone. Furthermore, some schools will give you academic credit or allow you to do an independent study on your business.

Scholarships/Awards/ Competitions

Description

Scholarships, awards, and competitions are often overlooked ways to invest in your tangible and intangible assets. Many students think that they have no chance to win anything. However, what many fail to see is that there is a wide variety of scholarships, awards, and competitions and how you brand yourself in the application has a huge effect on whether or not you win. Chances are that you can find one that matches your strengths and passion.

If you own your own business and have written a business plan, why not participate in a business plan competition? If you love fashion design and already designed a lot of outfits, why not submit them to a design competition? If you are or have done your own extreme endeavors, why not have your hard work validated!

Benefits:

1. **Money.** Ben Kaplan, a recent graduate, was able to get $90,000 through scholarships and pay for his whole education at Harvard. He has also authored an excellent book, called *How to Go to College Almost for Free.* Having your college education partially or completely paid for will provide you with the opportunity to graduate college with a

clean slate and begin your career debt-free.

2. **Branding.** You will be getting a credential that can be leveraged for future opportunities. In the same way that companies may look at an individual being accepted to Harvard as pre-screening, so may they also look at prestigious scholarships and awards. If people in the past have found you worthy of an award, the people you meet in the future will assume you must be talented.

3. **Networking.** Organizations often give awards not only to help students, but also to make themselves look good. When you win an award, the organization gains a vested interested in your success. The more successful you become, the better the organization or competition looks. Furthermore, many organizations also provide mentoring, networking, and further support opportunities.

4. **Development.** By applying to many scholarships, awards, and competitions you gain the valuable skill of understanding your target market (judges) and catering a product (yourself) to them. This skill can be easily applied to job and college admission processes!

5. **Growth.** Scholarships and awards often force you to ask yourself important questions that you may not normally ask. This process gives you a better idea of who you are and what you want to become. Of the successful scholarship applicants I have talked to, all of them cited personal growth as a major benefit.

Shadowing

Description

"Shadowing" an upper-level executive is a valuable opportunity to see what a company is like at the top. While internships can give you valuable hard skills, they only show you what it's like at the bottom of a company. By gaining a perspective of what the people are like at the top, you will be able to make better career decisions. If you do not like the lifestyle of the firm's executives, then what is the point of vesting years of your life to become one? You do not only have to shadow upper-level executives. You can shadow anybody who interests you.

Benefits:

1. **Credential.** Shadowing is respect-worthy, not only because it is a valuable and unique experience, but also because it displays pro-activity and creativity. Human resources departments do not often recruit people to shadow their busy senior-level executives, so getting in the door definitely shows skills they might value in somebody they might hire. Kevin Colleran, a student entrepreneur, shadowed billionaire John Malone, who is a very private person and difficult to meet. In a conversation I had with Kevin, he pointed out that people were very impressed that he was able to get in the door and shadow such a private and successful individual.

2. **Branding.** Your shadowing experience may change an individual's perception of you for the better. If you are shadowing a senior-level individual, you can drop his or her name when you meet new people. Having your name associated with somebody who is so successful, will improve your brand.

3. **Networking.** If you are shadowing an executive at the top of a corporation, you become more valuable to people, both inside and outside the company who want to build a relationship with who you are shadowing.

   You can use your position to network with others in the company. When I was shadowing Steve Mariotti, president and founder of NFTE, I would observe him as he went about his daily work. Often, people would come in to speak with him. If I did not know them, I was given an introduction, thus expanding my network.

   Shadowing individuals puts you on their radar screen. As such they are more likely to pass on resources that could be helpful to you. As you develop a relationship of trust and respect, they will be more comfortable giving you larger opportunities.

4. **Flexibility.** Because the person you are shadowing does not expect you to deliver results for the company, and is not paying

you, you have more flexibility as to when you shadow. Also, because there are generally low expectations on what you will accomplish, it is easy to exceed expectations by doing extra things. For example, with Steve Mariotti, I would help him organize his office and write proposals on how I thought the company could be improved.

5. **Development.** Though shadowing a senior-level executive does not allow you to develop hard skills, such as accounting or marketing, it does provide you with the opportunity to observe somebody at the top of a successful company, which can be very valuable. While what you learn may not be immediately marketable, you might learn effective communication or job strategies that could change the path of your entire career. Furthermore, you will learn how to act around senior-level people.

6. **Growth.** Internships and part-time jobs give you a limited, short-term view of a career path. What they fail to provide you with is an objective, long-term perspective. They do not answer questions about what your job and lifestyle will be in twenty or thirty years when you become very successful. Shadowing senior-level executives give will you a broader perspective. For example, I for a very long time wanted to be the CEO of a large company. After learning more about

what this would be like through shadowing, I'm realizing how stressful it can be and I'm rethinking my career.

Seminars/Conferences/ Organization and Association Meetings

Description

Seminars, conferences, and organization and association meetings are another category of overlooked Extreme Endeavors. Students are willing to pay hundreds of dollars for a credit, but in many cases are not willing to put the necessary resources aside for something that could be even more beneficial. During the first two years of college, what I learned from about 600 hours of seminars and conferences has made a significant impact on my life.

Benefits:

1. **Networking.** At seminars, conferences and other such events, you will have the opportunity to meet like-minded people. This can be beneficial because it is easier to gain value from those with whom you have things in common, and with whom you have a higher probability of maintaining long-term contacts. In many cases, you will be pursuing similar resources, so exchanging them will be mutually beneficial. For example, often when I go to seminars people there tell me about other seminars and opportunities that would interest me. Furthermore, the people who attend seminars are generally older. Thus they are

often impressed by a young person taking the initiative to attend and are willing to help him or her.

2. **Branding.** Going to seminars and conferences shows initiative, is unique, and therefore these unique events are valuable credentials on your resume.

3. **Experience.** Because so few young people attend these events, the value of the information received and differentiation from your peers multiplies. Seminar companies have to be good or they will not be profitable in the long run. They also have to constantly improve their products and services to keep ahead of their competitors. These can lead to a very powerful learning environment with information that is often far more up to date than you will get anywhere else. I have never been to a seminar that I regretted to going to.

4. **Personal Development and Growth.** Seminars and conferences are great ways to put yourself in an empowering environment outside of your daily routine. It is very rare to have the opportunity or discipline to focus on development and growth for long periods of time.

Strategic Volunteering

Description

As a volunteer, you don't have to donate your time and get nothing in return. You don't have to perform menial tasks for an organized event or organization. Instead, you can create your own where you see a need that aligns with your interests and goals. By strategically volunteering you can look at volunteering as an exchange in which you offer something in return for a non-monetary asset. By strategically volunteering, you will open yourself up to new opportunities to invest in your intangible assets.

Examples:

1. Giving away a product/service to an employer or client.
2. Starting or running a school club.
3. Serving on an advisory board.
4. Connecting people who could help each other.
5. Sharing information with people who need it.

Benefits:

a. **Brand.** Strategic volunteering can give you opportunities that you would not normally have. For example, if you are starting a company and you donate your services, it will be easier to get a client, exceed expectations, and build a track record. A non-paying client is often better than no clients at all when you are just starting out. A non-paying client will be more understanding and willing to help you out through referrals, testimonials, feedback, and advice.

People don't like to work with greedy people. By volunteering, you brand yourself as somebody who is willing to give back.

b. **Growth.** Volunteering feels good. Strategically volunteering for causes related to your vision feels even better and is an experience that can shape your worldview.

c. **Development.** Volunteering your products/services can be a valuable way to gain experience. Over the summer, I was a business plan judge for the National Foundation for Teaching Entrepreneurship. This experience allowed me to see, from a different vantage point, how I could improve my own future presentations.

d. **Network.** During my freshman year, I helped a successful executive coach complete her web site for free. Since then she and her husband have each sat down with me to offer advice and she has introduced me to her contacts more than once. More importantly, I now have a life-long relationship.

Mastermind/Junto/Salon

Description
Benjamin Franklin met weekly with a group of local business men from different industries in what is called a *Junto* (Spanish for "group"). Each week a member would write a paper on a specific topic that would then be discussed by the group. The meetings were taken very seriously. From these discussions came the concept of the fire station and the public library.

Napoleon Hill, in *Think and Grow Rich,* after studying some of the world's most successful individuals including Henry Ford and Andrew Carnegie, concluded that having a "mastermind alliance" was a major key to their success. He defines a mastermind alliance as "Two or more like-minded people coming together in a spirit of harmony and mutual growth to achieve a definite aim." It is extremely important to focus on quality people that you trust, that want you to succeed, and who are on a similar journey, so the right spirit of harmony is created. If the right spirit of harmony does not exist, then meetings can be a waste of time.

On a more practical level, your own mastermind alliance might mean bringing together a very close group of friends, committing to each other's success, and:

1. Giving feedback on strengths, weaknesses, and ways other members could improve.

2. Offering up your own goals, vision, beliefs, values, plans and ideas for feedback.

3. Sharing resources.

4. Communicating on a weekly or bi-weekly basis.

5. Discussing and debating topics that are important to all.

Benefits:

1. **Networking.** Participating in a mastermind alliance or junto will build your network in a crucial way. While you will not necessarily meet many new people, you will build relationships that are more meaningful.

2. **Development.** A mastermind or junto offers valuable feedback on yourself and your ideas that you may not have access too alone. It will give you support and new strategies with which to achieve your goals.

3. **Growth.** Participating in a mastermind or junto with like-minded people will expand your worldview in a way that learning on your own can not.

Informational Interviews/ Mentors

Description

Informational interviewing is an underutilized method of career and self exploration that involves meeting with targeted individuals who can help you achieve your goals. These people can help you by talking about their experiences, answering your questions, offering advice, sharing resources, and/or recommending you to other individuals for additional informational interviews and mentoring. Getting the interview is only half the process. When assessing the value of a mentoring informational interview, it is important to think about the potential. The more effective and mutually beneficial your interview is, the more willing the mentor will be to help you in the future and include you in his or her network.

Informational interviews often take place over lunch or breakfast, or during the day in the mentor's office. Since the people you will be meeting are often very busy, you will want to make it as easy as possible for them to help you.

When participating in this extreme endeavor it will be important to come thoroughly prepared to all meetings with a list of insightful questions and background knowledge on the person and the people/organization(s) they are affiliated with. Once the meeting is over, maintain the relationship by thanking the individual and keeping in touch with them.

Good places/organizations to approach about informational interviews are:

1. An organization's existing mentor network.

2. Office of Career Services at your school.

3. Individuals who volunteer at your school as speakers, mentors, or who in some other way demonstrate their commitment to young people.

4. Individuals that really inspire you or who you think could help you in a meaningful way.

Benefits:
1. **Networking.** Informational interviews give you the opportunity to meet and begin relationships with individuals from whom you can learn a great deal. You have chosen them for the value you believe they can offer you. Furthermore, informational interviews will allow you to meet contacts of contacts and thus expand your network exponentially.

2. **Development & Growth.** Mentors are a great resource for answers to questions, not only about your current pursuits, but life in general. These meetings are useful for learning from the mistakes and successes of other individuals, so you can avoid or achieve them respectively.

Journaling

Description

Journaling is another powerful yet underestimated tool. It involves writing down insights, musings, observations, lists, beliefs, values, pictures, goals, stream-of-conscious thoughts, and anything else that comes to your mind. Journals do not have to be written in a linear fashion or even to make sense. They will be for you, and not for somebody else, to evaluate. Leonardo Da Vinci, who is famous for his journals, might have a joke, a drawing, and a model of an invention all on the same page. Consider the following excerpt from Michael Gelb's *Discover your Genius: How to Think Like History's Ten Most Revolutionary Minds*:

> *In a classic study of mental traits of genius, Catherine Cox examined 300 of history's greatest minds. She found that geniuses in every field — from painting, literature, and music, to science, the military, and politics — tended to have certain common characteristics. Most notably, she discovered that geniuses enjoy recording their insights, observations, feelings, poems, and questions in personal notebooks or through letters to friends and family.*

Benefits:

1. **Development.** According to Win Wenger's book, *The Einstein Factor*, one of the most fundamental laws of psychology is the "law of effect," which states that every act reinforces itself. Therefore, every time you have a new idea and write it down you reinforce it. Subtle thoughts you may have never brought to

fruition, come to the forefront in journaling and improve creativity.

2. **Growth.** Journaling is a great way to organize your ideas. I have found journaling to be particularly effective for building and reinforcing my worldview, clarifying my thoughts, and expressing myself.

Vuja Daze

Description

"Vuja Daze" is a term that I once saw in a magazine article. It is derived, of course, from the French "déjà vu," the sensation of having seen something before, though you know you haven't. However, vuja daze, instead of having to do with memory, means to experience something new, out of your normal realm of activities.

Examples:

1. Travel somewhere you have never been.
2. Put yourself in situation where you can meet new people.
3. Learn a new language.
4. Move to a new place.
5. Read books and magazines you might not normally read.
6. Attend lectures, poetry readings, concerts, and other activities that stimulate your mind in new ways.
7. Start a new hobby.
8. Take the longer, "scenic route" home.
9. Expand your comfort zone by doing things you normally wouldn't do (sky diving, public speaking, starting a business, taking a semester off).

Benefits:

1. **Growth.** Vuja daze can be particularly beneficial because it expands your worldview. With an

expanded worldview will come the ability to make more informed, empowering decisions that will change the entire course of your life. Expanded worldviews also affect how you process and store new information. If your perspective is limiting, then a lot of information that you have stored will be as well.

Mother Theresa had been a nun for ten years, working with middle class children, and she herself was from a middle-class background. Her life changed suddenly when she experienced vuja daze. She saw a poor and very sick woman on the street and decided to help by taking her to a hospital, where she could receive proper medical attention. However, wherever she took the woman, she was rejected. Finally she sat down, holding the dying woman in her lap and let her go peacefully. It was at this point that Mother Theresa made the decision that she would devote her life to helping poor people.

2. **Development.** There is a saying that sameness breeds sleepiness. Have you ever had to do the same busy-work repeatedly and become tired and bored? Have you ever walked into a room with a strong smell, and then, ten minutes later, got used to it and forgot there was a smell? The human mind blocks out repetition and sameness. Incorporating vuja daze into your life means constantly challenging and stimulating your brain and expanding your comfort zone. It means consciously pursuing new experiences

that could add value to your life, no matter how "weird" they may at first seem, or how much they challenge you. When you engage in vuja daze, you are bringing energy and liveliness into your life.

Buying Real Estate to Live In

Description

After a seven month research study, Dolf De Roos, author of *Real Estate Riches*, concluded that there were two major qualities that rich people uniformly had in common. The first was that they all had integrity. The second was, "The rich either made their wealth, or kept their wealth, in real estate." Buying real estate is an often-overlooked opportunity for college students (depending on what college you attend). For many colleges, students have the option of moving off-campus. When students move off-campus, they rarely consider the option of buying instead of renting the apartment or house they will be living in. Instead of paying a large expense each month, parents and/or students could be making a profitable investment. By the time a student graduates, they could have a significant amount of money invested. They could either choose to stay in the same location, rent it to somebody else for additional income, or sell it and pay off school loans or other expenses. Also, having real estate near a university helps to ensure that there will be a constant demand for people to rent the premises.

Buying real estate to live in is certainly not for everyone. By buying real estate you take the risk of the local real estate market going down and not being able to keep up with mortgage and tax payments. Before you jump head first into real estate, I would recommend consulting with experts or reading some books on the topic.

Benefits:

1. **Money.** Buying a house or apartment while in college is a great way to leverage your money. For example, my girlfriend and I pay $1,150 per month for our one-bedroom apartment in Brooklyn as of the writing of this book (we are working on saving up money for a down payment). So, every year we pay $13,800 in rent. If we were to keep paying the same rent until we graduated, we would have paid a total of $41,400 and have nothing to show for it. If we had somehow been able to buy the apartment when we were first moving in instead of paying rent, we would have been paying taxes and the mortgage, which would in turn would have given us a good deal of equity in the apartment. Every month we would have been making an investment in the house and our ownership percentage would have been going up.

2. **Brand.** Buying a house or apartment at such a young age is a unique and exemplary achievement. It can be leveraged to get jobs, internships, scholarships, or demonstrate experience to investors in future deals.

3. **Development.** Learning about the whole process of buying real estate can teach you about saving money, negotiating, managing tenants, finance, and much more. These skills can be leveraged personally and professionally in the future to buy other real estate or to

achieve other goals.

Case Study:
Below is the inspiring case study of Michael Slate, a
student at Purdue, who was able to buy a four-unit
apartment building.

*During my sophomore year here at Purdue, I decided to rent
my first apartment. After the excitement of having my own
place wore off, I realized that I was paying $800 a month for
someone else's mortgage payment and had nothing to show
for the money I was spending on rent. I started studying the
real estate market in the area by looking at houses, talking to
neighbors, reading articles in the local newspaper, combing
the classified section of the local newspaper, and reading
every real estate magazine catalog I could get my hands on. I
was not spending a lot of time. Whenever I had a free hour or
so I would drive around. It only takes a few minutes per day
to comb the classifieds. After studying the local real estate
market, I realized that the time to buy a property in
Lafayette, Indiana was right away. Interest rates were, and
still are, very low, not to mention that everyone in Lafayette
seemed to be selling, making it a true buyer's market.*

*At that point, I began searching for a duplex, thinking I
would live in one side and rent the other side out. There were
hundreds of duplexes for sale in Lafayette and I was
determined to find the perfect deal. I used a method from
Multiple Streams of Income, a book written by Robert
Allen. His method allowed me to rate each property that I
looked at and decide whether to look further into the deal.
After about eight months and evaluating over 40 duplexes, I
was getting rather discouraged. Most of them were built
before 1950 and needed a lot of upkeep. Since I am a college*

student, I do not have a lot of time for maintenance. My search took a turn for the better when I saw an ad in the paper one day that said, "4-plex located in Lafayette, showing excellent returns and fully managed." The ad seemed too good to be true but I decided to still take a look.

When I arrived, I was immediately impressed. Not only was it less than five years old, but it was better than most of the other apartments in town. It had fireplaces, vaulted ceilings and included a washer and dryer. This place was definitely luxurious. Finally, I had found a place that I would not be ashamed of or scared to live in. The current owner gave me a copy of the financials and I was even more impressed.

To help me analyze the financials, I called David Hosei, a friend of mine, and the only guy I know that has more ideas than me. A thorough analysis showed that while living in one unit of the property I would have to pay about $200 a month in order to break even. Paying $200 a month and having ownership of a 4-plex sounded a lot better than paying $800 a month in rent for a smaller apartment. Plus, if I wasn't living in the unit and renting it out to somebody else, the property would generate $400 a month.

The only drawback was the fact that the seller was asking $245,000. "How could I afford that?" I thought to myself. Well, it turns out that the appraisal price for the property was $266,000. That was exactly the leverage I needed to afford it. Because the appraisal price was $21,000 more than the asking price, I had a $21,000 down payment, in the bank's mind. While doing research I noticed that, due to current economic conditions, most banks only wanted about 10% down. Because the purchase price was then $266,000, I *had to come up with a down payment of about $26,600 and borrow about $240,000 from the bank.*

At this point, I needed a $5,600 ($26,600 - $21,000) down payment. Because I was able to talk the seller down from $245,000 to $240,000, I was able to make an even smaller down payment. It seemed like everything was falling into place. The only problem was that, as I talked with banks trying to get a loan, I realized that by only putting 10% down, I would have to pay something called Private Mortgage Insurance, which was about $120 a month. This type of insurance protects the bank in case I stopped making payments. I basically felt that the insurance would be money that I would flush down the toilet every month. Therefore, I decided to figure out how to put 20% down, which would allow me to forgo paying the Private Mortgage Insurance. I was able to talk the seller into carrying a second mortgage of 10%, which meant that I would not have to pay the insurance and that I would have to pay monthly mortgage payments to the seller as well as the bank.

After talking to many different banks, and asking the brokers who the best banker was, I found one that would be willing to give me the loan. The amazing thing is that, when I got to closing, I only had to pay $625 out of my own pocket. It seems that the seller was responsible for pro-rated taxes and some other closing costs. The other neat thing is that my mortgage payments did not start until the month after I closed. By then I would be getting rental income. This meant that the $1750 I had set aside for the first month's mortgage payment did not have to be spent. So I put $1750 in my bank account, which I am saving for emergency repairs and months when the units are vacant.

The property is fully managed by a trustworthy management company. They take care of pretty much everything, from renting the units to mowing the lawn. They even deposit the check into my bank account for me. All I do is open the financial statements in my mailbox every month. When all was done and said, I had $26,000 of equity in a 4-plex worth $266,000 with no down payment on my part.

Saving Money

Description

Saving money is the act of putting money aside for future use. This is a simple and important concept that many people simply have difficulty carrying through (including the author). At first glance, you may wonder how a mundane activity as saving money can be an Extreme Endeavor. Just because it is simple, does not mean it is easy. In fact, the average middle-class 50 year old has paid $500,000 in taxes over a lifetime with only $5,000 in savings to show for it. In other words, people always find enough money to pay the government, but never enough to pay themselves. But why bother paying yourself, if you are not going to use the money until sometime in the future? Hopefully, the following thoughts will give you a new perspective on the benefits of saving.

Benefits:

1. **Development.** By putting aside a percentage of your income, no matter how small, you develop the habit of saving — a habit which most people never acquire. No matter how little you think you make, you will always have some amount of money that you can contribute to the habit of saving.

2. **Money.** Saving gives you a reserve of money. With this reserve you will have more options. If you are starting your career and find something that interests you, but it does not pay as much as

you would like in the beginning, you could afford to take such a job. Or perhaps you could even afford not to get paid for a few months. Saving also ensures that you can always pay your bills on time, establish good credit, and not be stressed out every month when you are just barely making your bill payments. Lastly, with a reserve you will have money to invest in opportunities as they arise.

3. **Growth.** By having more money than you need, you can reduce financial anxieties and focus on what is really important to you. Many of us spend too much time being forced to focus on what is not really important in the big picture.

Investing Money

Description

Investing money is putting money towards your tangible and intangible assets with the hope of a return on your investment. Which assets and liabilities you invest in are determined by your goals and your plan to achieve them.

When spending money, it will be important to differentiate between your needs and wants. Unfortunately, this can be difficult. When you are used to a certain lifestyle, good clothes, a cable TV, or a nice car, these *wants* become *needs* in your mind. As people increase their income, they have to pay more taxes and they often increase their expenses, because they confuse wants with needs. Over time, most people's wealth does not increase substantially, due to poor investment decisions.

One of the best ways to experience the difference between needs and wants is to assume full financial responsibility over your life. When you are spending your own money, but are having difficulty making ends meet, you look at the world differently. When I was a sophomore at NYU, I decided to take a leave of absence for a semester. My mother did not support this decision and, as a result, she cut the money she was giving to me for rent, food, and other expenses. I no longer had a school meal plan and I had to pay for rent, and all of my other expenses, myself.

Part IV: The Extreme Endeavor Curriculum

Based on the advice of a close family friend, I started keeping track of all my expenditures. To my surprise, I not only found I could reduce my expenses by 75%, my quality of life improved, because I was able to enjoy myself regardless of how much money I had. Instead of focusing on transitory external possessions, I concentrated on controlling my emotions internally. As a result, I am more able to control my state regardless of what is around me. Some of the decisions I made to reduce my expenses were:

1. Rent movies rather than go to theaters.
2. Don't buy new clothes.
3. Don't buy a TV.
4. Move into a less expensive apartment.
5. Don't buy new furniture for it.
6. Eat in and eat healthily. As a result of a healthier diet, I need less food to fulfill my body's nutritional and energy needs.
7. Find recreational and leisure activities that do not involve money.
8. Apply to scholarships for conferences to be able to attend for free.

It is very important to realize that more money does not necessarily mean a better quality of life and less money does not mean a lower one. In fact, according to the *Okinawa Program: How the World's Longest-Lived People Achieve Everlasting Health--And How You Can Too*, this island, not America or Europe, has the longest-living individuals. In fact, the residents of Okinawa routinely live independent and vibrant lives into their nineties and even hundreds. This example shows that having more money does not necessarily increase longevity, or the quality of life. While many people look at their diet as a need, they do not realize that they could eat less, save money, and be healthier. I maintain a mindset that allows me to differentiate between needs and wants and make wiser investments. In the past, I thought that people who did not spend all their money were missing the point of it. If you have more money, why not spend it to make yourself happier? Now I can see the value in being happy regardless of possessions. I also recognize the benefits of saving money.

By reducing expenses instead of increasing them, you will begin to look for ways to improve your quality of life that do not involve money. In *The Millionaire Next Door*, Thomas Stanley points out that the true "millionaires" are not the ones living in large houses with fancy cars. They may be your next-door neighbors who live humbly. The parents of one of my best friends have, in many ways, been second parents to me. They have always lived below their means. When I was growing up, I would sometimes wonder why they did not buy a bigger house or a fancier car. Now, I can appreciate the fact that they are very happy without depending on material possessions.

If your parents are supporting you, I would suggest testing yourself and improving your mindset by putting all the money you receive into some form of savings where you cannot touch it for a certain period of time. This would give you a perspective similar to one in which you were supporting yourself.

Part IV: The Extreme Endeavor Curriculum

Once you distinguish between your needs and wants, you will not need to depend on money to transitorily improve the quality of your life. Furthermore, you can align your wants with your assets instead of your liabilities. With a clearer picture of which expenditures will help you achieve your goals the quickest, you will be able to use your money more effectively.

Examples of Financial Investments:
1. Stocks
2. Real Estate
3. Business
4. Bonds
5. Certificates of Deposit
6. Savings Account

Benefits:
1. **Money.** Investing money leads to passive income, money you don't have work for. Once your passive income exceeds your expenses, you no longer have to work for your money at all if you don't want to.

2. **Development.** By learning how to wisely invest your money, you free yourself from worrying about it and learn how to leverage it to achieve your goals.

Taking Time Off

Description

From pre-school or elementary school, we go through more than a decade of schooling. Even after all this time, many communities look down on people who take a few months off. However, what we aren't taught in school is that taking time off can be a liberating experience.

Examples:

1. **Dropping out of high school and going to college.** Jubair Chowdhury, founder and president of Sybess Technologies (http://www.sybess.com) was having difficulty fitting his business and school together. From this frustration, he researched his options. His conclusion was that he would drop out, pass the G.E.D. (a high-school equivalency test), focus on his business for a few years, and then go on to college. I respect Jubair for making such a difficult and non-conventional decision.

   I also like this path because it bypasses "paying dues" (high school) and gives the opportunity to focus on what you are passionate about for a few years. I can imagine that by the time Jubair is 18, he will be far ahead of his former classmates, who were not able to focus on their passions. This strategy seems as if it would work best only for those who are highly motivated and capable of handling criticism. When making such a decision, it is obviously important to include your parents and convince them that your reasoning and future plans are sound — if you still want to live in the same house.

2. Break between high school/college, semester off, or break between college/career. Josh Bierne-Golden decided to take two years off before attending college. In his own words:

There were numerous reasons I took the semester off. I had been accepted to NYU Tisch for drama and was planning on attending right after high school. I was not really sure that I wanted to try to make a life for myself as an actor and at the last minute I decided to go to Brown as a creative writing major. It was probably the rashest decision I have ever made. My parents were really worried that I had rushed into a choice I might not have been ready for. They had encouraged me all along not go to college right after high school. At this point, though, I was adamant that I would go to Brown and all my problems would be solved. I am really grateful that they finally convinced me to start there in the summer instead of the fall.

When I got to Brown it was nothing like I expected and I was miserable. I finally realized what my parents had known all along: that I was not ready for college and that I did not have to go if I was not ready.

I had a great deal of both internal and external pressure to go to college right away. There is a section in the documentary "Bowling For Columbine" that sums up the way I felt perfectly. In the film, Matt Stone, who is one of the creators of the TV show South Park, talks about his high school experience. He explains that from the time we are in sixth grade, give or take a few years, we are taught that if you do not follow the traditional path outlined by society you are bound to fail and essentially are doomed to a life of poverty and loneliness. Nothing could be further from the truth. In reality, it is clear that it is people who create their own unique path who are most often successful. At the age of 17, while everyone you know is following this one way of doing things, it is almost impossible not to believe that it is the only way to be successful. Essentially, you are scared into believing it. In addition, I went to a high school in which the majority of my graduating class went on to junior college or simply found a job. As a result, having someone on their way to NYU or Brown was a great source of pride for my school, so I felt a good deal of external pressure as well.

How I was able to overcome it? I was lucky to have parents who were not only accepting of my wish to take time off, they actively encouraged it. Furthermore, I allowed myself room to make mistakes. I am a great believer in the fact that there are no right or wrong choices, you simply have to choose one path and, if you are unhappy on it, be unafraid to find a new one.

At first, taking time off was a lot of fun, maybe for a month or so. It was a bit of a novelty I would say. For the first time I could remember, it was September and then October, and I was not in school. When Thanksgiving and Christmas started rolling around, though, and I saw my friends from high school coming home from college and asking me when I was going to get on with my life, I started to feel really depressed, as though I was never going to do anything. It was tough going for a while.

I initially worked at my mom's office during the day and tried to keep up with tennis (at the time, it was tennis that I thought would be paying for college). I made a big push to rededicate myself to tennis and started playing more national tournaments. However, when college application deadlines were coming closer, I was still unsure of what I wanted to do, so I decided to take another year off. It was around this time that I found I was becoming more and more passionate about writing and I would come home every night and just write for hours, on and on, which is what eventually led me to pursue writing my play. The play took me and a year and half to write. Once I was done, I literally went from theatre to theatre in San Francisco dropping off copies with my name, address and phone number on it, hoping someone would buy it. I was very naive and someone easily could have stolen it. Within the first few days, one of the first theatres I went to called me and told me they were interested in buying it. I went in and spoke with them and a few weeks later I had a contract signed with one of the largest theaters in San Francisco, that had won a Tony for best regional theatre.

I would say almost everything that happened during the two years I took off was a positive. I helped my grandparents, gained work experience, really began to feel as though I was fulfilling my potential in tennis, and discovered how passionate I was about writing. The most important lesson I learned though was that not everyone has to take the same path through life. In fact, for some people, me for instance, following the path that everyone else did would have been catastrophic. The only negative was feeling depressed and directionless for a while but, in the long run, that only made it clearer what I was passionate about.

Benefits:

1. **Development.** I have spent the last 13 years of my life going to school. My only major breaks have been during the summers. Taking a semester's leave of absence helped me grow because I had to support myself for the first time in my life, with very little support from my mother. I had whole days open and had to fill them up with things to do. In essence, I had a lot more responsibility and I had to create my own life curriculum.

2. **Growth.** Taking a semester off is more than taking a few months off from college. It is the

choice of taking a non-mainstream path and this is why it is so difficult. Diverging from the main path is why business is more than simply selling services and products. It is why half of the journey is just beginning it. It is the difference between thinking something is cool and never doing it because you are afraid and diving head first not knowing where (or how) you will end up. If you have ever jumped from a high diving board at a swimming pool you will know what I am talking about. Even though you know that you will be landing in many feet of water, and if you dive correctly you will most likely not be hurt, you are still afraid. Do you have the courage to look at Extreme Endeavors the way you would jumping off a diving board? Do you have the courage to follow through with achieving a goal if it's important to you?

Taking a semester off gave me the opportunity to focus my energy on what is truly important to me at a core level. I had the opportunity to have "time on" over a period of many months. I have to say I think I have become addicted to placing what is important to me over what is easier. I have learned that I would rather struggle to make ends meet and do what is important than have security and follow everybody else. Therefore I never have to fear failing because I know, even if I fail, I will still be at a place where I can be happy.

Now, imagine this. Imagine a world where all

we are doing is putting time on. We are spending time with people who are important to us, doing what we were waiting our whole life to do, voraciously improving and growing, learning, playing life as if it were the best game in the world, with endless possibilities and options.

Leveraging School

Description
Mark Twain once said, "Don't let schooling interfere with your education." School can be a very effective way for you to accomplish your dreams. However, in my opinion, most people let schools use them instead of making school work for them. Everybody is different and has different goals, so everybody has a different highest and best use for schooling. Below are some of the benefits one can receive if he/she uses school to its highest potential. School can become an extreme endeavor if you maximize the benefits and minimizes the costs.

Examples
1. Appear on campus media and win student awards to improve brand among other students and teachers.

2. Join the executive board of club(s) that interest you the most.

3. Perform research with a professor.

4. Participate in study abroad program.

5. Actively look for events on campus that interest you and attend them.

6. Meet with great teachers after completing their class or even meet with teachers that you've

never taken a class with.

7. Research all of the resources your school has available to students.

8. Learn from alumni who got a lot out of school.

9. Make a significant commitment to finding the best teachers in your school.

Benefits:
1. **Network.** University networks are centers for business- and thought-leaders. Schools have access to mentor networks, successful alumni, like-minded students, teachers, speakers, and administrators, many of which have a stake in your success. Extreme Entrepreneurs actively meet people who can be very valuable to them and who are willing to help. For example, through NYU's Office of Career Services' Mentor Network, I was recently able to meet with an Emmy Award winning, senior correspondent for the WB11 News At Ten.

2. **Branding –** Whether we like it or not going to highly ranked schools improve your branding. At the same time, there are many ways to get around not going to a highly ranked school or going to college. As mentioned earlier, many successful individuals never graduated college.

3. **Growth –** Schools expose you to a lot of new ideas. By putting in time to learn about the best

courses and teachers, you can maximize your experience.

4. **Development** – Courses are not ends unto themselves. On the contrary, they mark the beginnings of intellectual exploration in different areas. Classes can help you find if you're interested in a topic so you can decide if you want to explore it more in the future.

Jobs and Internships

Description

Part-time jobs and internships are often used as opportunities to get credentials and work experience. However, they can be so much more valuable than that. They can be opportunities to move up in a company or get a full-time job where you can invest in your tangible and intangible assets. To receive this sort of opportunity, you will have to transform how you look at part-time jobs and internships. First, how you make decisions will be crucial. Some questions you may want to ask yourself are: "What opportunities will I have to move up in the company? How much will the person hiring me be willing to let me prove myself and help me succeed?" Once you are on the job, instead of counting the hours pass, you will need to find ways to over-deliver and exceed expectations. At an entry-level position or internship, this can be easy because expectations are low.

Examples:

1. **Compete with people 10 years older than you.** Kevin Colleran, a junior at Babson College and a successful young entrepreneur, was able to get an incredible summer internship at BMG, which then recruited him for a fast-track management program initially created for MBA students.

    Kevin was not offered the job because of grades or internships. He had never had a prior internship. The company saw that he was already experienced in the industry, and because he had a strong track record in the real world.

2. **Make the Most out of Internships.** Another individual, who prefers to remain anonymous, was able to take an internship and turn it into an Extreme Endeavor. While in college, he was able to get an internship by pitching his unique language skills to a leveraged-buyout firm that wanted to invest in the privatization trend in Europe. These companies purchase companies using debt as leverage. While on a trip to Poland, his native country, he saw a great opportunity. The Polish Government, at the time, was privatizing its industries and selling its assets. This enterprising student noticed a factory for sale at a great price, did the background work on the deal, and then showed the situation to his boss, who gave the go-ahead. The student orchestrated the purchase and made himself and the company he worked for a lot richer. Now in his twenties, he is a partner. He never had to "pay his dues" in the industry.

3. **Leverage Entrepreneurial Experience.** Alexis Bonnell started two successful businesses during high school and college. Leveraging the intangible assets from those experiences, she was able to get a job with the Association of Interactive Marketing. Within a few years, she

was promoted to director of marketing and her unofficial title was Digital Diva. When she decided to move on, she got job offers from a number of companies for executive-level positions. She eventually chose to become the president of Verbal Advantage (http://www.verbaladvantage.com), in California, which at the time had annual revenues of $12 million. She was 25.

Motivated undergraduates and recent graduates can follow similar paths of escaping having to pay dues or taking a job just for the money. To accomplish this, however, you will have to stray from the norm. You will have to create enough value for the company to prove that you would be more of an asset at a higher position. This is certainly not easy and especially difficult at larger and more established firms, which often depend on a set way of doing things with employees moving up the corporate ladder in a prescribed fashion. By working in a small company, you will be able to work closer to the top, and take advantage of a less stringent hierarchical structure.

Part V:
The Extreme Entrepreneurship Challenge

Everyone has superstitions. One of mine has always been when I started to go anywhere, or to do anything, never to turn back or to stop until the thing intended was accomplished.

— Ulysses S. Grant

13

The Challenge

*We must not cease from exploration and the end
of all our exploring will be to arrive where we
began and to know the place for the first time.*
—T. S. Elliot

The core challenge of Extreme Entrepreneurship is to
create a life where you can constantly participate in
Extreme Endeavors! Below are some challenges you
may want to consider in addition to your own:

- Buy a house or apartment while in college.

- Win a prestigious grant, competition, or award.

- Start a business.

- Develop a skill that you love and would do for free,
  but that can earn an income (e.g., Acting, Directing,
  Writing, Speaking, Singing, Painting or Sculpting).

- Shadow an interesting and successful individual.

- Get media attention (radio, T.V., print) for your
  accomplishments or what you are currently doing.

- Go to a seminar, conference, or association meeting.

Part V: The Extreme Entrepreneurship Challenge

- Start a journal.

- Take time off.

- Become financially independent before graduating.

- Strategically volunteer for a cause you believe in.

- Forgive anybody that you have not forgiven.

- Live in a very different culture.

- Subscribe to a magazine you never would normally.

- Have an informational interview with a role model.

- Shadow a person that you don't understand and learn what they're about.

- Learn how to build relationships with people who are different than you.

- Travel to a place you've never been to before.

14

The Journey

The most important part of work is the beginning.
—Plato

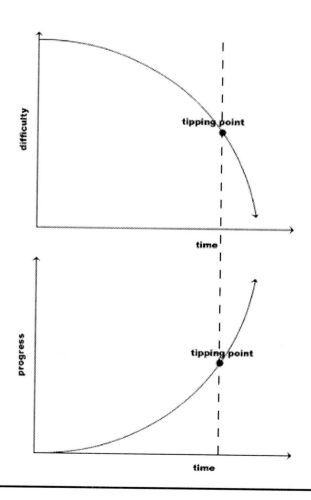

Part V: The Extreme Entrepreneurship Challenge

Consider the graphs above. Based on my experiences and what I have read, they demonstrate your journey, if you choose to follow the Extreme Entrepreneurship model. The lower graph shows how the beginning of your journey yields the least tangible progress. The upper graph illustrates how the beginning is the most difficult. Therefore, in the beginning, when it is most difficult to hang on to your magical dreams, it is most necessary to have patience, faith, and courage. From this model comes the saying that *The beginning is half the journey.*

The tipping point occurs when you have created a system of tangible and intangible assets that are doing the work for you. As you reach the tipping your progress accelerates. After all, the owner of the Laundromat down the street may work just as hard as Bill Gates. But because Bill Gates has a much larger system of assets, he has the potential to make more progress in much smaller amounts of time. Looking at the charts, you will see that the tipping point occurs when you reach a positive feedback loop from the choices you've made in the past. More progress occurs in smaller and smaller amounts of time and things become less difficult. This is a similar to a rocket taking off into outer space. While in the earth's atmosphere, the rocket must continually fight against gravity. However, as the rocket starts to leave the atmosphere and gravity decreases, it becomes easier and easier to make progress.

A beginning is consistently the most difficult part for people, and it is what I would like to now focus on. By straying from the norm, you will probably receive heavy external social pressure from those who love you the most, as well as dealing with internal fears and self-doubt, both of which will be encouraging you to keep within the norm. To successfully implement the Extreme Entrepreneurship philosophy, you have to be not only committed to the beginning, but the long-term journey. You have to be willing to overcome whatever stands in your path for your dreams — including yourself.

Before you start your own journey you should commit yourself to overcoming mental obstacles that arise, for they surely will. Don't feel that everything else in your life has to be perfect. Would you rather worry about how little time and money you have and how you need to get your grades up, or focus on investing in your long-term dream? Below is a checklist of obstacles you must mentally prepare for and commit to overcoming:

- Eliminate self-doubt.

- Eliminate procrastination.

- Eliminate fear of failure.

- Deal with constant external pressure to follow the norm.

- Prepare to work harder in the short term for less money.

- Prioritize freedom over security.

- Notice and abolish excuses that you realize you are making.

Questions to Ask Yourself

1. Do I have the courage to prioritize what I am passionate about and what I believe will help me achieve my long-term goals?

2. Am I willing to have my actions reflect my priorities?

3. Am I willing to go through difficult times in the present-moment and focus on long-term value?

4. Do I want to be extremely successful and a major agent of change of my time? Am I willing to do what it takes to be one?

The New Path

An interesting phenomenon that I have noticed among students is that they often know what they are passionate about and what they want to do, but they do not do it. For example, one young woman I spoke with had the dream of opening a coffee shop. However, instead of learning about how to run a coffee shop, she was investing in Plan B by learning about how to get into the finance industry so she could have a more "stable job," even though she was not interested in taking a finance major. If she is passionate about taking a certain career path, why couldn't she devote time to it in the present? Why wouldn't she follow her dream, a seemingly easy choice?

We live in a society where people put more effort into secondary plans (Plan B) instead of dreams (Plan A). Many individuals want to finish school, get high grades, and participate in the 'right' extracurricular activities that they may not be passionate about, just so that if they fail they will have something to fall back on. In other words, if they never get the chance to pursue what they *are* passionate about, they will have jobs that they are *not* passionate about to fall back on. According to an Associated Press article last year by Robert O'Neill, Americans in general are becoming less satisfied with their jobs. Below is an excerpt:

> ... *A 2002 survey of 5,000 people found that while most Americans continue to find their jobs interesting and are even satisfied with their commutes, a bare majority like their jobs.*

> *Only 51 percent were satisfied with their jobs, compared with 59 percent in 1995, the survey revealed...*

> ...*Job satisfaction increased with income levels, but even among the higher-earning households, it had dropped from 67 percent in 1995 to 55 percent in 2002, holding steady since 2000.*

I propose a new path, a path on which you focus on plan A (your passion) and that, by focusing on plan A, you will develop backup plans that you are also passionate about. How is this possible, you may ask yourself? It will be made possible by investing in tangible and intangible assets that support your passions. For example, let's say you are interested in opening a business and want to create a backup plan. Assets that you could invest in are:

- Brand: Developing a good reputation.
- Networking: Network with potential clients, investors, partners, and employees. Each new person you add to your network is part of another backup plan.
- Development: Learn as much as you can about starting a business, both in terms of theory and in practice.

You can never *guarantee* success. However, what you can do is increase your chances by expanding your options so that you can take advantage of more opportunities. Each asset you develop is a potential opportunity that you could fall forward onto.

For example, imagine someone who likes cooking and who has the dream of coming up with a new type of cuisine that will change the lives of the people that eat it. He could focus on plan A, which he is passionate about, by constantly cooking new meals and testing them out on people. Each time he cooks a meal he could learn something new. With that new knowledge, he would have an increased awareness of what works and doesn't, which would help put him in position for future success. Thomas Edison put this principle to work perfectly. When asked about the fact that he had thousands of failed inventions, he simply commented that he now knew thousands of options that did not work. Something that he did not mention, but that is also true, is that by testing so many possibilities he learned small things that *did* work. By investing in Extreme Endeavors you will constantly be creating opportunities for yourself that you can always fall forward on to.

In embarking on your own career, you must be willing to make the decision of whether you will follow the conventional or Extreme models. By following the latter, you will be choosing to take a path that may be more difficult in the short term, but extremely rewarding both in the short and long terms. In the Extreme path you must refuse to pay dues in a system you do not agree with. You must never settle for anything but Plan A, no matter how little time, money, or resources you think you have. You must be willing to do what you believe is right. No matter who you are, you can begin right away to invest in tangible and intangible assets that support your vision.

Never Settle

If you are committed to creating value, and if you aren't afraid of the hard times, obstacles become utterly unimportant.

> — Candice Carpenter, CEO, iVillage

We are confronted with finding lucrative work we enjoy, and that blends well with our family or social life. This can be difficult, especially in today's environment. Perhaps that is why so few students manage to do it.

Many students choose one priority (e.g., work) at the expense of another. This is a shame, because different assets are not mutually exclusive! If you want to make a lot of money, you can still do something you are passionate about, make a difference, and spend time with close friends and family. We are lucky enough to live in a system where this is possible. Earlier I stated the importance of blending instead of balancing. Here I will reiterate its importance. A person who can effectively blend makes statements like, "How can my social or family life help my career?" or "How can I find a career where I can utilize all of my assets?" "The late Thomas A. Edison freely admitted that Mrs. Edison was the major source of his inspiration. They held their Master Mind meetings daily, usually at the close of Mr. Edison's day's work. And nothing was permitted to interfere with these meetings."[11]

I encourage you to create your own path and not settle on one pre-made. When put in situations that you do not like, either get out of them or change your responses. *Do not settle.*

Which option would you choose? Plan A or Plan B.

If you are currently investing in Plan B and want to be investing more in Plan A, are you willing to give it priority? Are you willing to set everything else aside to invest in your dream?

No matter where you are, you can begin devoting more time to investing in your intangible assets and creating more backup plans. Think of every person you meet, credential you get, and skill you develop as another backup plan.

If you use school as a primary plan and focus all your time on it, you will become dependent on it. However, if you use school as a backup plan, you can leverage it and avoid being dependent on it. By leveraging the system, you can focus on what you are passionate about, whether the economy is up or down.

When an individual invests in school and dreams are a backup plan, the damage will not always be visible, but it will be there. Any second you spend not moving towards your goals and vision is a second where you cheat yourself. When given the choice between good and great, why not choose great?

15

Start Now: Youth
Competitive Advantages

You don't know if something is right or wrong until you try it.

Whether you agree or not with the points I have brought up in this book, I would like to challenge you to test your existing beliefs and be open to new ones. One suggestion would be to ask people you would not normally talk to for advice. More specifically, talk to people who have achieved the goals you aspire to without paying dues. If you can't talk to them, then read stories about them. If you talk to or read a story about someone who achieved such goals and *did* pay dues, they will almost surely say how important it was to pay them. Why not find a way to achieve your vision without prioritizing your secondary plan and paying dues?

Being young gives you many advantages in pursuing Extreme Endeavors that you may lose after you graduate. Some of these are:

1) **Networking.** When you meet people and or start your own business, you do not have to be perfectly polished. In fact, you are not even

expected to be. If you are ambitiously getting yourself "out there," the simple fact of your presence will make an impact and exceed expectations. Lou Markstrom, founder of Own America, says, "Doors that will be closed after college are open during college." So my question to you is, why not find those open doors now?

2) **Less Student Competition.** How many students do you know pursuing their vision and actively going to conferences, traveling, writing articles for publications, and starting businesses? There are certainly not many, which makes your story more press-, scholarship-, competition-, organization- and award-worthy. Accomplishments that seem incredible in college become only mildly impressive once you graduate.

3) **Resources that support youth.** There are many nonprofit organizations and individuals that focus on or support entrepreneurial youth. One such example is your school, which can be a very powerful tool to leverage. It is your job to surround yourself with people who can, want to, and will help you succeed.

4) **Secondary Stream of Income.** Many college students are lucky enough to receive some sort of consistent support from their parents. If it is not consistent, then it is at least something they know they can fall back on. If their venture fails,

they probably will not be starving and homeless. Also, because their expenses are lower, they will not need as high an income to support themselves as fully self-supporting adults do.

5) **School Environment.** There are many resources that schools can provide beyond the courses and professors you are personally familiar with. Your school might have departments related to what you are doing. Furthermore, you may be able to get funding for your business, research, travel, or conferences through your school. Professors have office hours (a.k.a., free consulting) where you can ask them questions beyond what they talked about in class. You are in an environment surrounded by people your own age. If you are proactive, you can probably find at least one person who is on the same page as you are.

6) **Blending School and Extreme Endeavors.** Your business or other Extreme Endeavor can help school, and vice versa. Some schools will allow you to receive academic credit, or perform an independent study with your project.

7) **Flexible Schedule.** No matter how busy you think you are, your college years might be affording you more free time than you will ever have, until you retire. When you think about it, all you have definitely set in your schedule are your classes. Beyond that, you might have extracurricular activities, studying, and so on,

but they take variable amounts of time and you can often do them just as easily at 9 p.m. as you can at 1 p.m.

8) **Flexible Spending.** College is a unique environment because, probably for the first time in your life, you will have money to spend on whatever you like. Because you are so far from home, you do not have to tell your parents exactly what you are buying. Also, you will have a schedule flexible enough to earn money on the side. Instead of spending the money going out several times a week, you may want to plan what you really want and save for it. Instead of purchasing items that may or may not be bad for your body and are gone the next day, why not purchase things that will be with you for the rest of your life, or at least while you are paying off the debt. As Robert Kiyosaki says in *Rich Dad, Poor Dad*, "Have your money work with you and not against you."

9) **Reduce Your Costs.** College is a great time to learn how to spend less rather than worry about small differences (e.g., $9 or $12) in income from jobs/internships. However, if you are paying interest and late fees to credit card companies, and buying things you really do not need and can't really afford, then it does not matter if you are making $9 an hour, or $12. Reducing your expenses will give you the option to get a job that earns less and that adds value to your life.

10) **Creativity.** Young people have a fresh perspective on the world. This viewpoint lends itself to seeing opportunities that have not yet been exploited. The founders of Microsoft, Yahoo, Dell, Fed Ex, and Napster all saw unique opportunities and capitalized on them when they were still students.

11) **Less Corporate Competition.** Many entrepreneurial opportunities open to students are, at first, not profitable enough for corporations to consider. For example, Sean Fanning created Napster out of his dorm room at Northeastern University. Napster never earned a profit and is now bankrupt, yet I am sure Sean does not regret a moment of it, considering the intangible assets he gained through starting the company. When starting a business, student entrepreneurs have fewer personal costs and therefore can charge their customers less. This is a competitive advantage both against larger, established companies and adult start-ups.

The Real Decision

Now that you have read this book, you have the tools to make a massive change in your life. If you have not already begun, my first question is, "What is stopping you?"

Many different reasons may immediately have popped into your head. Even though I do not know what they are, I suggest that most of them are secondary or irrelevant. They are limiting you now as they probably have done so in the past.

This book is not about succeeding or failing, it is about trying. It is through this process that you can compare what is inside your head with what is actually true. I do not recommend blindly following the concepts I have brought to your attention but I do recommend trying them. By trying a new idea, you will be able to find what does or does not work for you and thus you will be able to develop a more complete worldview. You will never have to say, "What if?"

On this note I urge you to begin your new journey. As Dr. Martin Luther King, Jr. said, "The time is always right to do what is right."

Join the Movement

The Student Success Manifesto is just one part of The Extreme Entrepreneurship Education Corporation (E.E.E.C) curriculum. Beyond this book, I have begun to work on other products that will help my readers fully assimilate what they have learned, and take action. Please visit http://www.successmanifesto.com to learn more about our products and how you can become part of this grassroots youth movement where young people begin following their own journey paved with their own values, beliefs, and goals.

Pass It On

If you liked this book I would ask you to take a few moments to suggest it to anyone you think would benefit.

Newsletter

Also, if you liked what you read and would like to receive my free newsletter updates and opportunities on topics related to Extreme Entrepreneurship, please send your e-mail to michael@successmanifesto.com with "Subscribe" in the subject line (I will never give out your address).

Feedback

Feedback is always helpful. I would appreciate it if you would share your thoughts (positive or negative) about the book with me. My email address, again, is michael@successmanifesto.com.

Endnotes

1. Mathew Lesko, *Free Money to Change Your Life*, Omaha: InfoUSA, 2001.

2. Tony Robbins, *Unlimited Power*, New York: Simon & Schuster, 1986.

3. The Power of Entrepreneurship – *Fast Facts*: http://www.ncoe.org/entrepreneurship/fastfacts.html, 2002.

4. Jeff Gates, *The Ownership Solution*, New York: Perseus Books, 1998.

5. Linda Lee, *Success without College*, New York: Broadway Books, 2000.

6. Mathew Lesko, op cit.

7. Robert Kiyosaki, *Rich Dad's Guide to Investing*, New York: Warner Books, 2000.

8. Steve Mariotti, et al., *The Young Entrepreneur's Guide to Starting and Running a Business*, New York: Random House, 2000.

9. Jeffrey Timmons, *America's Entrepreneurial Revolution: The demise of Brontosaurus Capitalism*. Babson College, F.W. Olin Graduate School of Business, 1998.

10. Marilyn Kourilsky, *Seeds of Success: Entrepreneurship and Youth*, Dubuque: Kendall/Hunt Publishing Company, 1999.

11. Napoleon Hill, *The Master-Key to Riches*, New York: Ballantine Books, 1965.